THE BUDDHIST BEAT POETICS OF DIANE DI PRIMA AND LENORE KANDEL

By Max Orsini

Published by Beatdom Books

Copyright © 2018 by Max Orsini

All rights reserved. No part of this book may be reproduced in any form or by any electronic or mechanical means including information storage and retrieval systems, without permission in writing from the author. The only exception is by a reviewer, who may quote short excerpts in a review.

View the publisher's website:
www.books.beatdom.com

Printed in the United Kingdom

First Print Edition
ISBN 978-0-9934099-5-0

PREFACE

A pronounced spiritual and aesthetic interest in the East has pervaded American cultural, intellectual and aesthetic thought since the mid nineteenth century. From the Transcendentalists to the Modernists, the Harlem Renaissance writers to the Beats, American authors—and poets, in particular—have engaged in a number of imaginative conversations with Eastern religions; however, no discourse has proven more pervasive than the American-Buddapoetic one initiated by Beat Generation poets of the 1950s and 1960s. As a result of the work of poets like Diane di Prima and Lenore Kandel—the two authors who serve as the focus of this spiritopoetic book—Buddhism has become a sacred muse in contemporary American poetic discourse, and has proven to be a catalyst for a turn toward language as sacred ritual in American poetry after WWII. While indeed a great deal of scholarly attention has been traditionally paid to male authorial engagements with Buddhism, the twenty-first century has proven a fruitful epoch for examining female contributions to Buddhist literature, and female and male scholars, critics, literary-historians and poets like Diane di Prima and Lenore Kandel have worked to (re)vise, (re)define, (re)imagine, and (re)interpret poetry, culture, and identity through a Buddhist lens. This book seeks then to meditate upon ways American female poets Diane di Prima and Lenore Kandel have fundamentally shaped the form and content of American Buddhist poetics by meditating deeply on the nature of human suffering and by utilizing the consecrated space of poetry as a means to minimize human anguish. More specifically, this dissertation will contemplate the literary and artistic, mytho-spiritual quests made by two unique women writers of the Beat Generation who, like Buddha, have courageously journeyed into the depths of the human mind, heart, and spirit to liberate themselves, and others, from individual and collective samsara in search of personal healing, creative freedom, and spiritual reawakening.

TABLE OF CONTENTS

INTRODUCTION:
A New Geography of Consciousness:
American Buddhist Poetics and the Arrival of
the Blue-Light Dakinis—Diane di Prima and Lenore Kandel ... 1

PART ONE:
Spirit from Sense:
Diane di Prima's Zen Broth Simmering ... 53

PART TWO:
Unlocking the Golden Gates:
Lenore Kandel's Big Beat Buddhism
and the Opening of Emerald Consciousness ... 119

CONCLUSION:
Rugged Road, Open Hand, Swinging Door:
Essences of an American Beat Buddhist Poetics
and the Mantra of a New Generation ... 197

WORKS CITED ... 211

ACKNOWLEDGEMENTS

*Deep thanks to my mother,
for believing in me,
and language's power to liberate us from bondage,
and to my father,
who has helped unfold a map of possibility.*

*Many thanks also to Professor Peggy Samuels,
whose piercing vision shimmers through
and Professor Liana Piehler,
whose brushstroke care emanates out.
You have been Dakinis on this road.*

*And, of course, to Nikki,
the emerald muse enduring:
dhanyawādāh, dhanyawādāh, dhanyawādāh*

INTRODUCTION

A New Geography of Consciousness

American Buddhist Poetics and the Arrival of the Beat, Blue-Light Dakinis—Diane di Prima and Lenore Kandel

"Whether we are aware of it or not,
something of Buddhism pervades American consciousness."

Diane di Prima, from "Conversations" with Timothy Gray

"California, for the early writers,
was both a place and a state of mind."

from Michael Davidson's
The San Francisco Renaissance: Poetry and Community at Mid-Century

Luminosity "Behind a Bright Screen": A Revolution of the American Spiritual Imagination between Two Wars

In the near thirty years that elapsed between the bombings of Hiroshima and Nagasaki in August of 1945, and Saigon's fall to Communist forces in April 1975, American literature experienced a plethora of revolutionary spiritual, political and aesthetic changes as its young writers, poets, musicians, painters, and soul-searching readers turned their eyes east toward Asia—in the directions of India, China, and Japan. With a reinvigorated, but turbulent fermentation of political orthodoxy and spiritual conservatism pervading American society in the years following WWII, a yearning for personal freedom and creative elasticity led to burgeoning swarms of writers on the intellectual and spiritual move—budding authors exploring new terrains of imagination and previously unexamined horizons of artistic and religious expression across the United States. Like the late teens and early 1920s, which saw a boom in both the American economy and a rise in literary output following WWI—leading henceforth to flourishes of writing from the Lost Generation and novelists and poets of Harlem's artistic renaissance—the climate of the forties and early 1950s was blustery with the ambivalent winds of cultural and aesthetic change blowing in the wake of military success abroad. However, while the Modernists of the twenties turned their glances toward Europe—many of them selecting Paris as their literary *axis mundi*—for many American writers after the Second World War, new centers of American artistic inspiration emerged in places like Kyoto and Tibet. Some authors-turned-soldiers or marines like the half-Jewish, half Christian, Vedanta-enthused, and Zen-meditating J.D. Salinger, returned from the war off the coast of Normandy with the drafted chapters of a soon-to-be celebrated *Catcher in the Rye* in his war-torn rucksack (Shields and Salerno xv-xvi). As 1950 dawned and Zen public intellectual Alan Watts delivered his Buddhist-inspired, *The Wisdom of Insecurity: A Message for the Age of Anxiety*, Salinger followed Watts' footfall on the way to his own Zen-inflected response to the atomic age in his 1953 collection, *Nine Stories*, which depicted characters like war-veteran Seymour Glass whose very words emanated a Taoistic slant of light. Indeed, American literature was witnessing a new chapter in its narrative architecture, as Buddhist impulses manifested themselves in its rapidly evolving artistic and cultural imagination.

Like Salinger, poet, painter, and eventual City Lights Books owner, Lawrence Ferlinghetti—himself a participant in the D-Day events at Normandy—was experiencing his own revolution of religious, political, and aesthetic consciousness. However, unlike Salinger, the northeasterner through and through, Ferlinghetti (whose own "political convictions took a sharp turn to the left" when he visited the desecrated city of Nagasaki just six weeks after the bombing) moved west to San Francisco in 1953 (Tonkinson 305). Like fellow Italian-American, New York poet, Diane di Prima, he made the Pacific city his permanent home. Ferlinghetti illustrates the impact the move made on his spiritual and literary consciousness when, in his poem "Confessional," featured in Tricycle's anthology *Big Sky Mind: Buddhism and the Beat Generation*, he remembers that in post-war California he "saw" something "new," "shining," something "spun in the sun" inspired by his reading of the "vajra lotus diamond heart" [sutra] which was "too luminous too luminous / to [even] cast a shadow," unfolding "another world," "behind bright screens" (Ferlinghetti 49-51, 61-67). To be sure, Ferlinghetti was not the only American writer experiencing this "luminous" manifestation of glittering-"diamond" "lotus"- unfurling consciousness by the mid-fifties. Undeniably, Buddhism seemed to provide, for America's Beat novelists and poets, a compassionate answer to the silent, brooding questions that lingered in the aftermath of a noisy atomic war. These writers were beat down, worn out by the persistent threat of greater political conservatism and the prospect of a future episode in the global drama of atomic warfare; however, they were also jolted by the beat of a more spontaneous, creative song, one whose bop tablature manifested itself like a new jazz calligraphy in the ears and eyes of poets and readers, and on the printed pages of bright, Beat books.

It was first in New York, and then, later, more forcefully, in San Francisco—where the West Coast juts out into the blue Pacific across from Asia—that another renaissance emerged. in which writers like Rexroth, Olson, Duncan, Kerouac, Ginsberg, Corso, Snyder, McClure, Whalen, Welch, Kaufman, Lamantia, and Ferlinghetti witnessed something new "spun in the sun," something spiritually "luminous" coming up on the eastern horizon. A new geography of consciousness was emerging; a new poetic ethos (as Ginsberg has often called it) was taking root in Catholic Saint Francis' Golden Gate City, and like Buddha, this group of writers was calling the earth to witness its enlightening inception. For as Ferlinghetti recalls in his retrospective Foreword to *The Collected Poems of Philip Lamantia*, it was the mid-fifties and it was ten years after the war in Europe had ended. Military service had uprooted so many Americans, many of whom returned home briefly, but didn't stay long. And a great migration of my generation began. It was as if the whole continent had tilted, and the population slid westward. It took a whole decade for the disparate elements of post war America to coalesce in a radically new culture. And it was happening in places like San Francisco...and North Beach. San Francisco was still a last frontier where a new world was aborning. (xix)

The stunning image Ferlinghetti provides here of a continent tilting and a population sliding westward is a significant one. For one thing, it highlights the migratory motif that pervades American literary history, this mid-century Beat migration west recalling the migration of African-American writers traveling from the American south to New York in the late teens and 1920s. Like the black writers and musicians, from whom the Beats received a great deal of inspiration, the Beats were searching for political and personal freedom; however, unlike the black writers of the twenties for whom a migration north signified a clear flight from an oppressive history of physical enslavement, the Beats moved west seeking a less particularized emancipation. In a sense, New York's Beat writers like Ginsberg, Ferlinghetti, di Prima, and Kandel traveled west in the '50s and '60s in order to discover what it in fact was that they wanted to be free *from* and what it was they hoped to find out in California. Like participants in the Gold Rush, a century earlier, the Beats saw glimmering streets and shimmering new lives, but for the

Beats, "gold" bore no monetary connotation. They were envisioning a golden gate bridge over American troubled waters, a place where they could "loaf and invite their souls," as Whitman had, and as Hart Crane had, a generation earlier in Brooklyn. The golden road west was instead a middle path to the heart of the human spirit, a trail lined with lotus flowers and brimming with the rush of awakening.

Beat Visions of Spiritual Awakening in the Golden Gate City on the Fringe

For Beats, the predicament was in fact not altogether distinct from that of early Puritan settlers who sailed west from England in search of religious tolerance and a terrain on which to explore their own nexus of faith three centuries earlier. However, markedly unlike those early American settlers, these mid-twentieth century poets and prose writers seemed to turn away from constricting notions of time and space, gender and sexuality, divinity and daily life. It was in Zen San Francisco that the Beats were able to slow down the pace of life in order to accelerate the speed and activity of their energetic enthusiasm for the world's diverse religions and cultures. San Francisco was, moreover, a place to actualize their imperative of widened artistic, environmental, psychic, and planetary awareness. In California, there was a sense of "life lived moment to moment as it unfolds," and that attracted Beat writers as John Clellon Holmes once told Beat essayist and biographer, Anne Charters, in a letter he sent her across country years after many of the Beats had moved from New York to San Francisco (Charters xxv). It was a group of "cerebral young men and women, too, I'm sure,"

Clellon told Charters with a bit of hesitance in that letter, young writers "attracted to the spontaneous, the impoverished, the random, thus the wondrous...to everything beyond the pale, outside the firelight, everything that has escaped the circumscribed" (Charters xxv).

Taking the Beat spiritual and cultural imperative a bit further, Kerouac famously told Mike Wallace in a 1958 interview that the spiritual force propelling the Beat Generation was "nothing less" than "a revival prophesized by [Oswald] Spengler" in his 1918 book *The Decline of the West* (Elwood 165). As Kerouac reported, Spengler forecasted that "in the last moments of Western Civilization, there would be a great revival of religious mysticism" (165). "It's happening," Kerouac continued to tell Wallace:

> Yet also: What I believe is that nothing is happening.... We're an empty vision—in one hand... [God] is the name we give it. We can give it any name. We can call it tangerine...god...tangerine. But I do know we're empty phantoms.... And yet, all is well. We're all in heaven now really. (165)

Kerouac's multi-layered explanation of the Beat "awakening" reflects the way in which Beat writers not only embraced what they recognized as a "great revival of religious mysticism" in the face of societal decline, but also emboldens Clellon's notion of immediacy, of something "unfolding", "moment to moment," right here and now in the vastly possible, "empty," and urgent, Zen present. Indeed, this vision of the immediate, of existence manifesting itself as an event, or a sequence of "happenings" not only reflects Kerouac's deep foray into Buddhist thought when he "ensconced himself in the San Jose Library" reading Dwight Goddard's *A Buddhist Bible* in the spring of '54, but it also reflects how steeped Kerouac and other Beat writers really were in Buddhist philosophy by the mid-fifties (Prothero 2). Certainly, budding Beat poet Lenore Kandel must have seen or heard the interview with Wallace in '58, prefiguring her own move to the West Coast in 1959. Kandel, whom Kerouac would later fictionally portray in his novel *The Dharma Bums* as "Ramona Swartz"—"a big Rumanian monster beauty of some kind...intelligent, well read, writes poetry, a Zen student, knows everything..."—stood, at least in Kerouac's sprawling mind, for everything that Beat spiritual exploration and literary experimentation would come to signify throughout the 1960s (Prothero 269). Meanwhile, in her Greenwich Village apartment back east, Diane di Prima was reading about D.T. Suzuki's own sense of Zen (in books provided by her Zen choreography teacher, James Waring) when she tuned in to listen attentively to Kerouac's and Lamantia's interview with Mike Wallace (Grace and Johnson 90). Surely, di Prima, a voracious reader in her own right, would have caught Kerouac's nod to Auden, who, eighteen years earlier, in his 1940 Memorium to W.B. Yeats, posited that poetry's spiritual power lay precisely in its ability to "make nothing happen" to make "emptiness" sing. Indeed, poets, eastern aspirants, and astute listeners would have all collectively heard the Taoist/Zen innuendoes in Kerouac's urgent, yet composed recognition that a "tilt" toward a newly blossoming spirituality which could not be "named" was indeed stirring fervent in the air by the late fifties.

But by the 1960s, windy San Francisco had become the nucleus of a "new consciousness" where new attitudes about poetry, self, and community were taking root, and writers from Haight-Ashbury to North Beach were listening closely to a Buddha who insisted that "each one [should] embrace his own truth / And devote himself to its fulfillment" (Maitreya 45). San Francisco, with its marginal cartographic location, standing outside the long shadow of eighteenth-century, European Enlightenment thinking, was a city where writers could go to lose themselves, to shed Euro-constructed identities, to release themselves from the total bondage of rational thinking, and find "fulfillment" of another sort. In a sense, San Francisco, for many truth-seeking poets of the fifties and sixties, was out of ego's reach, and to male poets like Snyder, Kerouac, and Ginsberg and newly blossoming female poets Kyger, di Prima, and Kandel, the Bay area was a locus of authenticity and unconditioned spiritual potentiality. As Michael Davidson observes, "The city [San Francisco] is a good place to be alone, the myth goes, and there are plenty of others with whom to be alone together" (Davidson 8). This quote encapsulates with exactitude the way in which San Francisco was able to spiritually and artistically serve poets in search of both solitude *and* community. In San Francisco, these self-identified "others" could become anonymous enough to find a meditative space in which to write and then ultimately become nationally recognized, as Kerouac, Ginsberg, and the Beats were on the evening of the famous San Francisco Six Gallery reading of 1955, when Ginsberg first shared his "Howl" of revolutionary compassion with the world. Indeed, San Francisco was "both a place and state of mind" for poets after WWII. On one hand, the city itself, which, for writers of California's past, signified an "untouched wilderness"—"a fall out of Paradise" rather than a New England Eden— was a place of "undeniable physical beauty" whose "position at the edge of the continent, its hills, its quickly shifting weather patterns and its wild seasons" made it the ideal locale for a literary movement championing creative spontaneity, verbal edginess, Indian and Japanese imagistic sensibilities, and a belief in cosmic flux (7). For these writers, "the fact of living in the west" meant "living at the margins, whether politically, religiously, or in extreme psychological states" (11).

A Poetic Sangha at the Heart of the Margin:
Women on the Edge of Consciousness

Given the still significantly marginalized position of women writers at mid-century (not to mention the pronounced marginalization of women in general within the domestic spaces of their own homes) it makes sense that poets Diane di Prima and Lenore Kandel would take to the road, heading west to write their names boldly in the left margin of the nation's literary narrative. Joining Ginsberg, McClure, Whalen, Kyger, and Snyder out west, di Prima and Kandel lived in close physical and aesthetic proximity to a group of Zen outlaws and hip-outcasts who, together, sat meditative, thought kinetic, and waxed poetic at the fringed threshold of literary truth. As Marianne Dresser, author of the anthology *Buddhist Women on the Edge: Contemporary Perspectives from the Western Frontier* might say, the Beat Generation was not only a confluence of Eastern spiritual currents absorbed by American male writers on the Pacific Coast; it was also a "cross section of American women's experience, perspectives from the fertile margins of the dominant discourse" (Dresser xxii). From there at the heart of the geographic, political, sexual, and aesthetic margins, di Prima and Kandel were able to, in di Prima's own words, "trade far memory" and "knowledge of ritual and suffering," take "hashish that smelled like the earth of some ancestral land" that "crumbled," "in hand" and, "without hesitance or guilt," find a "Road" less traveled that led from "Vision to further Vision" (di Prima xiv). This powerful recollection from di Prima's "INVITATION TO THE JOURNEY: Homage to Lenore Kandel," manifests both the bond that these writers shared as they lived together, dwelling on the "edge" of America—on the far margin of literary consciousness and the far fringes of themselves. There, in San Francisco, in the distant West, di Prima and Kandel "traded far memory" and shared insights central to the revitalization of poetry as a ritual practice where their egos "crumbled" like "earth", "in hand", only to expose with greater clarity the "big sky" of poetic potentiality and imaginative possibility that their Zen teacher Shunryu Suzuki Roshi believed to lie before them. For it is from the margin, from the edge of American society and poetic convention, that the "view is panoramic, clear, less obstructed by received knowledge or codified notions of correct views. It takes courage to stand on the edge and to speak," and these female Beat poets did just that, using meditation, silence, sisterhood, poetry, and even drugs, when necessary, to chant their disruptive, healing, seeking, unveiling, piercing, ritual language "with courage" from the "far" fringes of the American "frontier" (Dresser xxii).

To recognize the extent of these women's personal and poetic "courage," traveling around California in what Diane di Prima remembers as Lenore Kandel's "downtrodden pickup truck" (Knight 279), we need to pause for a moment, as Brenda Knight implores us to do— to "place their accomplishments in context" in order to "understand" why "any man or woman" in the "seemingly idealized fifties" and early sixties of "comfort and capital" would "choose to live marginally, to struggle and oppose" (3). "Postwar America," Knight continues, "was the richest, most powerful nation in the world, bustling with industry, pride, and the Puritan obsession with work and perfection. Or so it seemed" (3). On the contrary, female Beat poets like di Prima and Kandel were, according to Knight,

> some of the first to very vocally and artistically decry American materialism and conformity…. The[se] women…were talented rebels with enough courage and creative spirit to turn their backs on "the good life" the fifties promised and fought their way to San Francisco [and] made their own way…. In many ways women of the Beat were cut from the same cloth: fearless, angry, high risk, too smart, restless, highly irregular. They took chances, made mistakes, made poetry, made love, made history. Women of the Beat weren't afraid to get dirty. They were compassionate, careless, charismatic, marching to a different drummer, out of step. Muses who birthed a poetry so raw and new and full of power that it changed the world. Writers whose words weave spells. Whose stories bind, whose vision blinds. Artists for whom curing the disease of art kills. (Knight 3-4)

Knight's highly descriptive portrait of women-writers who bravely and "restlessly" wrote and traveled against America's post-war, sociopolitical grain is important in the way that it sheds light on the real struggles women like di Prima and Kandel faced in the fifties and sixties and how willing they were to get their hands—or feet or mouths—"dirty" in an age when women were expected to remain immaculately prim and clean. Additionally, San Francisco's Beat scene absolutely constituted what Gary Storhoff and John Whalen Bridge would call an "imagined community" of American Buddhist poets who sought to re-fashion American literary history by rebelling against "canons of taste" (1). Furthermore, Knight's portrait of Beat women emphasizes the equally significant fact that there was indeed a "high risk" taken by women who chose to swim against the stream of conventional society. The risk lay, in fact, in being further marginalized, in potentially becoming invisible, as it was for Diane di Prima, who dropped out of Swarthmore College after one semester in the early fifties, choosing instead to live on her own, first in New York's Greenwich Village, and then later, in San Francisco's Haight-Ashbury district. Di Prima's own story, much like Kandel's, can be seen as emblematic of a generation of women writers who refused to comply with the dominant hegemonic narrative and instead "birthed a poetry so raw and full of power," Knight contends, "that it changed the world" for women who followed them. By unbinding themselves from the glue of normative culture, di Prima and Kandel were able to tell new "stories" and write fresh poems that could "bind" women, and men, together, while also "blinding" readers with the fierce and Kali-like, prophetic force of their piercing insights into history, society, culture, femininity, racial and special struggles, Buddhist incantatory "vision." In the words of both Kandel and di Prima (as we shall see later), Beat women wrote a spiritually far-reaching poetry that "never compromises," one that is achieved "by any means necessary."

And yet, still, the question remains: how did they do this? Who were the teachers, literary influences, and spiritual catalysts that aided these women writers in the full realization of what Storhoff and Whalen Bridge, in *The Emergence of American Buddhist Literature*, would call a "pluralistic poetics"? (9). From whose hands did these female Beats receive poetic offerings of emerald awareness and blue-light wisdom? Which tongues helped them sing their dakini-songs as they wandered over land toward the Pacific to discover for themselves what Buddhism, poetry, and sisterhood had in store for them in the city by the bay? If Sharin Elkholy is correct in her assessment that "in various ways, Beat writers introduced Americans and their readers to new beginnings, new mythologies, and new frameworks of self-understanding" through "spontaneous and dynamic modes of expression," then where did these new "beginnings" of "self-understanding" and these emerging mytho-spiritual "frameworks" take root? (2). Which literary foremothers and forefathers helped di Prima, Kandel, and the Beats "capture" their unique "ethos of intensity, vitality, excess, and enthusiasm"? (2).

The Search for "El Dorado": Emerson, the Concord School and the Transcendental Roots of Beat-Light Consciousness

The earliest progenitors of Beat interest in Eastern literature and spirituality were, by all accounts, the American Transcendentalist writers who comprised the Concord School of Philosophy—namely,

Ralph Waldo Emerson, Bronson Alcott, and Henry David Thoreau, though to this list we must also add Walt Whitman, who we might consider, along with William Blake, the great inspiration of Beat literary vision and "cosmic consciousness" (Versluis 71). A century before the Beats "looked for Buddhist teachers," both at home and abroad, these Zen-countercultural artists "adopted an Emersonian ethos of self-reliance and a Thoreauvian appreciation of solitude in nature, many of [whom] went beyond books and embarked on a contemplative path by taking jobs—as loggers, sailors and fire lookouts—that placed them in the midst of nature" (Prothero 5). Though neither Diane di Prima nor Lenore Kandel worked in the woods or out at sea, an emphatic insistence on working "self-reliantly," outside the sphere of academia has indeed characterized a majority of their vocational lives. Though neither of these poetesses worked as a "logger" or "lookout" (as Gary Snyder for instance did), and though neither served in the U.S. Navy or the U.S. Marines, (as Kerouac and Ferlinghetti had), both di Prima and Kandel definitively embodied a Thoreauvian ideal, "transcending" gender boundaries of the time by working as performers in private theater companies, chief editors of small literary magazines, performing as belly dancers, serving as school bus drivers, and singing in community choirs, in addition to numerous other odd, but significant jobs at the societal margins. Only di Prima, who, in 1974, along with Allen Ginsberg and Anne Waldman, founded the Naropa Institute at Boulder, Colorado (now the Jack Kerouac School of Disembodied Poetics at the nationally accredited Naropa University), worked summers as an instructor of writing and Zen poetics (*Pieces of a Song* 199). In fact, di Prima now teaches writing on a strictly private level—her own pedagogical practice of self-reliance—preferring instead to work with students individually, rather than in large groups (*Pieces of a Song* 200). It might even be fair to say that no Beat writer has so fully embodied the Thoreauvian ideals of reclusion and introspection as Lenore Kandel, who lived virtually detached from the literary world for over twenty-five years, before eventually reemerging, albeit briefly, for the publication of Brenda Knight's book *Women of the Beat Generation*, thirteen years before Kandel's death in 2009 (Grace and Johnson 261).

For the Beats though, Transcendentalism provided more than a vocational, or even mythical, ideal. To be sure, writers like Emerson, Alcott, Thoreau, and Whitman were some of the first in American history to expose America to the spiritual light streaming in from Indian, Chinese, and Japanese spiritual tracts and literary texts. As Stephen Prothero observes, "The Beats succeeded in picking up the thread of the Transcendentalists in the wisdom traditions of the East and in nature and began to weave it seamlessly into the fabric of American life" (5). Interestingly, much in the way that Beat poets were misidentified and misunderstood by hegemonic America throughout the 1950s and '60s, Transcendentalists, too, were sometimes ostracized by a public who failed to recognize the creative potentiality that lay in the Concord Group's receptivity to ancient, eastern religious ideas. In fact, even Emerson himself, a former Unitarian Minister who read a significant amount about Buddhism and Hinduism in the vast library his father William bequeathed to him upon his death, initially expressed his own degree of ambivalence about Hinduism's overwhelmingly "immense goddary" and Buddhism's apparent "negative" sensibilities (Fields 57). Nevertheless, in spite of his admitted hesitations about the East's philosophical and spiritual paradigms, Emerson told his Aunt Mary, after graduating from Harvard, in a letter written in 1822, that he was indeed "curious to read" her "Hindoo mythologues," evidence that Emerson's deep immersion in Indian philosophy at Cambridge had richly awakened an interest in the East already budding early on "at the age of fourteen" (56).

"Even at his most critical moments," Rick Fields tells us, when Emerson found himself daunted by the apparent "misery of Asia," he "saw something else," something innately illuminating, as Ferlinghetti, Kerouac, Kandel, and di Prima later did, in India's deep spiritual history, eventually referring to India as "El Dorado," for the golden wisdom that it appeared to emanate from its seemingly endless vault of mystical forays into the unknown (56). Emerson, meditating on the significance of India's many visible philosophical contributions to the world, reasoned that "If the unknown was not magnified, nobody would explore. Europe would lack the regenerating impulses, and America lie waste had it not been for El Dorado" (57). Though initially, it would be tempting to read Emerson's comments here from an Orientalist perspective, treating Indian wisdom and philosophical insight as an impetus for the exploration or colonization of unknown lands—and this may indeed be somewhat merited—a more careful examination of Emerson's language here yields a tone of homage and an ethos of cultural inheritance rather than a championing of western imperialism sponsored by centuries of eastern philosophical inquiry. What Emerson is really acknowledging, in the aforementioned quote, is a degree of debt owed to Indian spiritualists and thinkers who had worked to make transparent those deep human truths often "hidden in plain sight," to borrow a phrase from the late David Foster Wallace (*This Is Water* 131). Additionally, considering the post-Puritan, Unitarian ministerial context from which Emerson emerged, it is not surprising that an admiration for being able to articulate that which might be deemed linguistically or socially "out of bounds" within early New England civilization would manifest itself in Emerson's widening philosophic and poetic consciousness. It is, most importantly, the "regenerative" spirit within India's cultural and philosophic traditions—its faith in earth or nature as a participant in creation and an agent to human enlightenment, its belief in reincarnation and karmic return, and its vision of a world comprised of interdependent living organisms working cooperatively—that Emerson no doubt picks up on here (and in his reading at large), for it is precisely that impulse of continuous creative rejuvenation and imaginative generativity that characterizes both Transcendentalist and Beat literature, the latter even more noticeably influenced by Hindu devotional practices and Zen beliefs in art as a manifestation of the spontaneous present.

Emerson was indeed beginning to sound more Beat, which is to say less Unitarian, and more like the pluralistic-Platonic-Hindu-Buddhist-Transcendentalist that he would later become by 1830, when his ideas about man, nature, and the divine prefigured an inevitable break from the Unitarian church. (Some critics like Rick Fields, for instance, have suggested that the catalyst for this break from the church was the "unexpected death" of his wife Ellen in February of 1831 (57)). After his wife's passing, Emerson, meditating on the nature of death, commented on the way in which the passing of a "dear friend, wife, brother [or] lover," "somewhat later" becomes an agent of "genius" and "assumed [for him] the aspect of guide" which "operates revolutions in our way of life" culminating, eventually, in a "growth of character" (57). Later on, in his journal from 1831, an increasingly more "revolutionary" sounding Emerson, who exclaimed, "congregations and temples and sermons—how much sham!," soon began to adopt, in his own words, a worldview centering more on the "divinity of man" than "the divinity of Christ" (57). Emerson concluded that passage from the 1831 journal, Fields certifies, "in any language a Buddha would have recognized," one in which, Emerson claimed, "the origin of self must be perceived" (57). Fields' work here on an eastward-turning Emerson, not only sheds light on Emerson's development as a quintessentially democratic "American" thinker in one of America's early stages of hybridizining, polymorphous thought; but it also prefigures the ways in which Beat writers like di Prima, Kandel, Kerouac, and Ginsberg were expressing a double "revolution" of the interior and the exterior—the spiritual and the political—where ideas about spirituality and politics coincided in a new American ethos of pluralistic self-reliance and self-seeking a century later, following WWII. Additionally, Fields helps us recognize the ways in which western writers and poets in particular have utilized Buddhism—traditionally one of Asia's most pacifying religions—to radically revise their own personal and aesthetic lives, and disrupt the social, political, and artistic architectures of a world they deemed unjust, or ethically uninhabitable.

Just as the Beats did over a century later, in a moment of intense personal and religious crisis in which he found "little love at the bottom" of the church's "great religious shows," Emerson turned to Buddhism, a religion he had initially thought of as both "negative," and "cold," for clarity, compassion, and apparent consolation. As

Rick Fields points out, Emerson had in fact "replaced a personal god for a more universal one," and had, in the Concord poet's own words, come to conceive of "prayer" not "as a means to effect a private end," but rather as a vessel through which to recognize that we exist "in the lap of immense intelligence which makes us organs of its activity and receivers of its truth" (58). Indeed, Emerson's turn away from a "private" god in conjunction with an emerging Transcendentalist zeitgeist that the Concord school dubbed "the Newness," was the natural anticipator of an American countercultural movement of the 1960s in which the "spiritual atmosphere of the new generation was eclectic, visionary, polytheistic, ecstatic and defiantly devotional" (248). Therefore, when the Beats arrived on the scene by the middle of the twentieth century, Buddhism (as well as Hinduism) had evolved from a "curious mythologue" to a permeating, sociocultural movement that captivated the depths of the American spirito-aesthetic imagination. It evolved from a budding "Newness" to a flourishing "New Consciousness," within the course of a century.

A Poetic "Passage to India": Walt Whitman, Asia, and the Birth of American-Poetic, "Cosmic Consciousness"

If indeed the Concord School's sense of a "Newness" stirring in the air of the mid-nineteenth century anticipated the Beat Generation awakening of a "New" spiritual, political, and aesthetic "Consciousness" by the middle of the following century, then certainly that Concordian sense of the "New" was more deeply and richly cultivated by the chief inheritor of Emerson's legacy, Walt

Whitman. While indeed Whitman may not have been totally facetious in 1857 when he responded with surprise to Thoreau's claim that his work was "wonderfully like the Orientals" (Whitman asked Thoreau to "tell" him "about them") literary and historical signs point to the contrary (Oldmeadow 65). For as Oldmeadow informs us, even Emerson felt the light of India emanating from Whitman's blend of spiritual and colloquial poetry, telling his friend, the writer F.B. Sanborn, that *Leaves of Grass* was "a mixture of the *Bhagavad Gita* and the New York Herald," an astute description of a poetry that fused mysticism and journalistic reportorialism as though they were intended to be married in verse (65). Elaborating on Whitman's own encounter with India and its literary and sacred texts, Harry Oldmeadow tells us:

> It may be true, as scholars have it, that Whitman did not own a copy of the *Bhagavad Gita* until the English cork-cutter Cockburn Thomson sent him one as a Christmas gift in 1857, but this hardly means he had not read it. There is Whitman's own statement in *A Backward Glance* that in preparation for his great work [*Leaves of Grass*] he had "absorbed...the ancient Hindu poems" along with Shakespeare, Ossian, Aeschylus, Homer, Sophocles, and Dante. Like Thoreau, he had read them out-of-doors, "probably by better advantage for me than in any library or indoor room—it makes such a difference *where* you read," he [Whitman] said..... It was...probable that Whitman read the Orientals, and swallowed them whole, along with everything else. While Emerson and Thoreau

> liked to use quotations from the Orientals like they were precious jewels carefully set in the main stream of their work, Whitman embraced them all and plunged into a kind of ecstatic eclecticism that swept everything before it (65).

Without claiming total or absolute certainty about the degree of Whitman's engagement with the East, Oldmeadow tactfully and engagingly weaves together some important threads in the loose narrative concerning Asian influences in Whitman's writing. For one thing, Oldmeadow allows us to see the ways in which Whitman extended the foray into Eastern writing previously initiated by Emerson and Thoreau. Yet, more importantly, Oldmeadow also calls our attention to the way in which Whitman's engagement with Asia was an apparently more profound one, a more intimate one that surpassed "jewel"-like quotations and extrapolated pearls of wisdom from the "stream" of ancient, Eastern thought. Indeed, there is the sense, both in Oldmeadow's critical assessment, and in Whitman's own leaves of verse, that an immersion in Indian spirituality is taking place, as is evidenced in poems like "Passage to India," where Whitman "turned from the New World he was always striking out for," to celebrate the "greatness" of India's "literary and spiritual past" (66).

For if, in the opening quatrain of his poem "Brahma," Emerson was more obliquely calling on the wisdom of the *Gita* when, he karmically mused that "If the red slayer think he slays, / Or if the slain think he is slain, / They know not well the subtle ways / I keep, and pass, and turn again" (qtd. In Oldmeadow 26), Whitman certainly prefigured a more definitive Beat immersion in the quest to revive a sacred Eastern past when, in "Passage to India," he ecstatically chants the following lines in three of the poem's inciting stanzas:

> ...first to sound, and ever sound, the cry with thee O soul,
> The Past! the Past! the Past!
>
> The Past—the dark unfathom'd retrospect!
> The teeming gulf—the sleepers and the shadows!
> The past—the infinite greatness of the past!
> For what is the present after all but a growth out of the past?...
>
> Passage O soul to India!
> Eclaircise the myths Asiatic, the primitive fables....
>
> Passage to India!
> Lo, soul, seest thou not God's purpose from the first?
> The earth to be spann'd, connected by network,
> The races, neighbors, to marry and be given in marriage,
> The oceans to be cross'd, the distant brought near,
> The lands to be welded together. (Whitman 8-15, 28-33)

These fourteen lines, extracted here from Whitman's 236-line, exalted ode to "infinite," India, "teeming" with clarifying or "eclaircising" possibility (Whitman here interestingly chooses the more Victorian, Francophone-sounding version to dignify the verb), collectively represent a major thematic and linguistic moment in American poetic history, and in the evolution of East-West literary studies at large. In the first pair of lines, we can hear Whitman's "Soul" (can we call it an extension of the Emersonian, universal "over-soul," here embodied in one speaker's voice and vision?) "cry[ing]: out for a "fable[d]" "past" in which the seemingly "unfathom[able]," "retrospect" of a more "primitive" human history can be illuminated by Indian wisdom and the unifying "Asiatic myths" of bygone days. Though he does not mention the *Gita*, the *Upanishads* or any of the "diamond, lotus," Buddhist Sutra (as Ferlinghetti called one of them a century later in "Confessional"), the turn to ancient Indian text is "eclaircised" both through the passionate intensity with which the poet speaks of India in the poem's stanzas and by the ways in which critics like Oldmeadow and Fields have pointed to Whitman's direct contact with Hindu and Buddhist texts. The lines from "Passage to India" feel charged with an energy acquired from consecutive hours of ecstatic reading "out of doors," turning leaves of sacred pages over in a globally-expanding, American mind.

Perhaps more significant than the poem's expansive, exalted, soul-seeking Transcendental vision, is its definitively pre-Beat poetic diction and its sense of limitless or "infinite" imaginative geographies and cosmic possibilities. Surely Harold Oldmeadow is correct when, in *Journeys East*, he posits that the lines from "Passage to India" contain "reminiscences of Blake and anticipations of Ginsberg" in their incantatory diction and their language of revelation (Oldmeadow 28). Not only in the anaphora initiating consecutive lines or the swirling, backward moving repetition of the phrase "the past"—both literary devices that come to characterize Beat poetry written by Ginsberg, Kandel, di Prima, Ferlinghetti, and others—but also in the very words Whitman selects in the poem.

Through its east-infused diction, "Passage to India" indeed serves to create a literary "network" linking Blake and the Romantics to Ginsberg and the Beats, as well as "Asiatic" literature to the literature of the west," through the wide "passage" of poetry. Even more specifically, the poem allows us to recognize the way "an oceanic feeling" (as the Emerson-inspired psychologist of religion, William James, called it) gets transmitted across history's "oceans" of humanity, through the canals of poetry's far-reaching geographic consciousness. The "oceanic feeling," according to James, is a feeling characterized by an elongated moment "when everything comes together, oneself, everyone else, the world, and divinity; it is like the feeling that we get when we stare out at the infinite reach of the ocean: it is a little frightening, but it is also awe-inspiring and exhilarating. As human beings we seem to seek out this kind of experience" ("In the Great Beyond"). Indeed, Whitman has this feeling in "Passage to India," and in numerous other poems as well, where deep in his bones he experiences the various "races" of the earth merging as a unified "network" within a cosmic web of life, across what he calls "measureless oceans of space" in his poem "A Noiseless Patient Spider." Here, in "Passage," words like "gulf," "infinite," "network," "oceans, "neighbors," "distant," and "lands" are evidence of a poetic mind capable of bridging geographic and political gaps, spiritual and poetic "gulfs," much in the way that Kandel's was, or di Prima's still is.

Richard Maurice Bucke, Arthur Versluis informs us, may have after all been correct then, when, in his 1901 book on Whitman, titled *Cosmic Consciousness*, Bucke proclaimed that just as the Vedas, the Torah, the Gospels, or the Quran were to ancient civilizations, "*Leaves of Grass* [would] be to the future of American civilizations" (Versluis 72). For Bucke, Versluis proceeds to say, Whitman stood for "an evolutionary advance toward individual and collective enlightenment. Whitman inaugurates what will become a familiar theme in the late twentieth century: that of religious evolution" (72). Hence, both for Bucke and for Versluis, Whitman "introduces the conception of the individual as a divine democracy of essences, powers, attributes, functions, organs—all equal, all sacred, all consecrate to noble use, the sexual part the same as the rest, no more a subject for mystery, or shame, or secrecy" (72). Versluis therefore not only helps illuminate Bucke's important turn-of-the-century prognostications about the enduring potency of Whitman's verse, but also renders himself in agreement with Oldmeadow, believing that Whitman "really is the ancestor of the late twentieth century modes of thought that we will see not only in the poetry and prose of Allen Ginsberg and the Beats," but also "in the counterculture" and the subsequent "phenomenon of twentieth century western gurus" (75).

Nevertheless, while the literary historical "networks" critics like Fields, Oldmeadow, and Versluis forge between Transcendentalism and Beat Generation writing are indubitably valuable to the advancement of East-West Studies and the "evolution" of Buddhist American Poetics, there exists virtually no scholarship which seeks to draw lines of spiritopoetic symmetry between Romantic or Transcendental, eastern-conscious writers, and female poets of the fifties, sixties, and seventies in America. More specifically, there appears to exist little visible published scholarship which illuminates, for instance, the powerfully overt and enriching literary connectivity between Whitman and Lenore Kandel, or Thoreau and

Diane di Prima, for that matter. Just as Whitman introduced a unique and previously unheard, unseen voice and vision into the American nineteenth century, along with an outlook of racial openness and an attitude of artistic receptivity into contemporary consciousness, so too did Kandel and di Prima introduce a distinct attitude of embracive, collaborative, poetic-sisterhood into the still somewhat white, male chrysalis of the 1960s cultural and ideological metamorphosis. As we will see later in this book, Kandel's Buddhist-inspired "Enlightenment Poem" is one that distinctively bares the "boot-soled" footprints of her "ancestor" Whitman's "Song of Myself." Yet, it is worth pausing for a moment now, to hear the way in which certain lines from Kandel's poem bare a deep spiritual and linguistic resemblance to lines 30-33 of Whitman's "Passage to India." Notice the way the following lines from the aforementioned poem by Kandel seem to coexist or coincide with those from Whitman, in a spatial geography of poetic consciousness that stretches luminous across a century of temporal shadow. Searching the cosmic "past" for an "enlightened," harmonious link between all of the universe's creatures, Kandel insists:

> we have all been brothers, hermaphroditic oysters
> bestowing our pearls carelessly
>
> no one yet had invented ownership
> nor guilt   nor time. (1-4)

And Whitman, dreaming of an Indian "network" of codependent origination among the species of earth, sings of

> The races, neighbors, to marry and be given in marriage,
> The oceans to be cross'd, the distant brought near,
> The lands to be welded together. (31-33)

Though Kandel's "Enlightenment Poem" directs its attention to the scientific "evolution" of the human "race" from its earliest origins, and Whitman's own enlightenment-seeking "Passage to India" more directly emphasizes the social unification of humanity over time, what the two poems share is a deep commitment to a democratizing spirituality that ultimately culminates in a dream of universal brotherhood beyond racial, creatural, and spatial division. It is not surprising that Kandel, who, according to Kerouac, "read everything," would have read, studied, and embodied Whitman's language enough to either consciously or subconsciously absorb his language, voice, vision, and spiritual ethos within the rich, mystical verbal landscape of her own poetry. Also audible in the space shared by the two poems is a distinctly Buddhist belief Kandel shares with Whitman that "ownership"—be it of lands, people, or things—is an illusion human beings cultivated to perpetuate contrived ideas like security and non-contingent individuality. By "non-contingent individuality," I mean a notion of individuality completely divorced from the world to which one inherently belongs as an atom or co-dependent molecule within the superstructure of the larger species. Never, when Whitman "sings of himself" in his poetry, does he do so as an "I" divorced from humankind. This is precisely why here, in "Passage to India," in "Song of Myself," and in numerous other poems, Whitman conceives of a world in which "races" of "neighbors" can "marry" or "be given in marriage." This definitively democratic, Buddhist sentiment echoes time and again from within the meditation chambers of American poetry. If Kandel's yearning for a race of "brotherly" human beings undivided by material and political notions of "ownership" is not enough to confirm the potent generosity of Whitman's spiritual, political, and artistic "offering" to twentieth century letters, then certainly Robert Frost's bitingly ironic axiom that "good fences makes good neighbors" will serve—by potent contrast—to affirm Kandel's agreement with Whitman, the sangha-seeking bard.

Eastern Images from the Modern Metropole: Pound, Imagism, and Zen Poetry beyond the Library's "Hard, Wooden Chairs"

If Stephen Prothero is correct in his assessment that "unlike the Transcendentalists, whose Asian religious interests remained largely textual," that the Beats "translated" Concordian "intellectual curiosity about Buddhism into actual practice," then how, within the short span of one century, did this "translation" or transition take place? (7). How did American Buddhist Poetics, from the pre-antebellum period to the period following the Second World War, experience such a rapid immersion in American artistic thought? To be sure, increasing American political interests and military involvement in the East will supply one answer, as evidenced by the growing participation of American writers in armed combat abroad. Undoubtedly, another answer to this question, as we shall discuss later, is the growth in the number of Japanese Zen monks and Indian contemplatives around the turn of the twentieth century traveling through, and settling in, the United States. However, while these political and religious developments do indeed figure significantly in the rise of American Zen poetics, these occurrences alone cannot entirely account for the inevitable rise of a new Asian poetic consciousness by the middle of the twentieth century. So, how then, did the move to a "practice" of Buddhist poetics occur?

Undeniably, the answer to such a question can be found by undertaking a brief investigation of the role that Modernist, Imagistic poets like Ezra Pound, H.D. Wallace Stevens, and William Carlos Williams played in absorbing aesthetic ideas that were historically fundamental, if not quintessential, to Tang and Sung Dynasty Chinese and seventeenth, eighteenth, and nineteenth century Japanese aesthetics. Modernist writers like Pound, H.D., Williams, and Stevens—as well as Yeats, Eliot, Archibald MacLeish, and even Marianne Moore, turned to the Far East during WWI at a moment when a "cultural crisis engulfed the European intelligentsia," as the "epochal event," the Great War was taking full swing (Oldmeadow 28). With an aggressive, inhumane war in "full swing," Asian literature offered a literary example of elegance without decadence, a distinct sense of formal unity without the overshadowing imprint of the poet's own aesthetic or personal consciousness upon the space of the poem. As Alan Watts eloquently points out in *The Way of Zen*:

> Since "one showing is worth a hundred sayings," the expression of Zen in the arts gives us one of the most direct ways of understanding it. This is the more so because the art forms which Zen has created are not symbolic in the same way as other types of Buddhist art, or as is "religious" art as a whole. The favorite subjects of Zen artists, whether painters or poets, are what we should call natural, concrete, and secular things. Even when they turn to Buddha, or to the Patriarchs and Monks of Zen, they depict them in a particularly down-to-earth way. Furthermore, the arts of Zen are not merely or primarily representational. Even in painting, the work of art is considered not only as representing nature, but as being itself a work of nature. For the very technique involves the art of artlessness, or what Sabro Hasegawa has called the "controlled accident" so that paintings are formed as naturally as the rocks and grasses which they depict. (174)

I quote the passage from Watts in full here because it paints an exquisitely luminous theoretical landscape for understanding what Zen art seeks to accomplish, and that is something quite "concrete" indeed. Watts' definition of the Zen artistic project, which centers on the Japanese avant-garde painter Hasegawa's phrase, the "controlled accident," elucidates precisely what Pound and his Modernists accomplices were after. Indeed, if we think of some of the most quintessentially imagistic works of the Modernist period—Pound's "Station of the Metro," H.D.'s "Sea Rose," Williams' "Red

Wheelbarrow," Stevens' "Snowman," Moore's "Egyptian Pulled Glass Bottle in the Shape of a Fish," and even certain moments of Eliot's "Preludes"—we become immediately cognizant of ways in which Modernism embraced a poetics grounded-in-nature, an austere and composed, but also vibrant, rainwater-glistening, modest Buddha who sat down close to the soils of the witnessing earth. Just as William's minimalist, lyric "Wheelbarrow" is perhaps a poem that deals more with the mind's ability to focus, as it were, its own attention, so is Stevens' "The Snow Man," Robert Aiken Roshi observes, less about a "construction of snow with two pieces of coal for eyes," than it is "a man who has become snow" (Aiken 69). "A snowman is a child's construction," Aiken goes on to say, in his essay "Wallace Stevens and Zen," but a "Snow Man is a unique human being with "a mind of winter," or, as Yasutani Hakuun Roshi used to say, "a mind of white paper" (69). In other words, just as a "mind of white paper" for a Zen monk or Zen aspirant might signify both a mind of complete contemplative control and unmitigated receptivity to the possibility of some spontaneous happening, so, too, is a "mind of winter" like a canvas unimpeded by psychic intrusions and temptations of formal disarray. A "mind of winter," "washes words clean" (as Williams famously suggested) and places its trust in the axiom that there exist, at least in principle, "no ideas, but in things," receiving creative inspiration from the very world that lies directly before it in "plain" sight.

Assuredly, Modernism—with its embrace of Zen's chief aesthetic axiom of the "controlled accident" served as a vital artistic "middle way" between the Transcendentalists' more textual, theoretical engagement with Eastern religiosity and the Beats' markedly more practical and poetical absorption of a Buddhist dharma poetics in the 1950s, '60s, and '70s. Though some critics choose to highlight the aesthetic dissimilarity between Modernist poetry and Beat poetry, the distinction is, more often than not, a misdirected one. For it was William Carlos Williams, descendent of Whitman in his own right, who, in his Introduction to Ginsberg's "Howl" (for Carl Solomon) powerfully wrote, "It is the poet Allen Ginsberg who has gone, in his own body, through the horrifying experiences described from life in these pages" (8). From this short, but evocative quote, we can see that Williams, at least by 1956, had come to recognize that, though there were indeed "no ideas, but in things," a poet's life could *also* be a "thing," a dynamic and poetically provocative ritual event, well worth "washing" and "waxing" upon in pseudo-sullied pages of post-atomic, poetic America. Indeed, the Jersey-born Ginsberg, and his friend, the Brooklyn native, Diane di Prima, were, in their early writing days, heeding the advice of the Imagist poets who were imploring them, in a dark time, to absorb the clear-seeing ethos of Chinese poets like T'ao Chien, Weng Wei, Po-Chu-I, Tu Fu, Li Po (whom Pound had translated), and Han Shan (whom Gary Snyder later emulated and translated) (Smith 11). Along with American translations of the more philosophical, but still highly poetic, Chinese wisdom texts like Lao Tzu's *Tao Te Ching* and the *I Ching*, (the latter, is in fact, the subject of one of Diane di Prima's earlier poems), these Chinese poets influenced American writers—Modernist and Beat alike—with their "intimate voices and outlook[s] centered in concrete things within a sense of life's Oneness" (11). Smith's observation here, simple as it may seem, is a valuable one, because it allows us to understand the way in which, despite their differences,

Modernist Eastern Imagists and Buddhists Beat Poets were in fact respectively searching for a "sense of Oneness" following WWI and WWII. Nevertheless, if pressed to recognize dissimilarity between these two literary movements, we can confer that what distinguishes their respective quests for "Oneness" is the fact that the Modernist quest was catalyzed by a search for Zen-like aesthetic unity as an end in itself, while the Beat foray was propelled by what we might call a "seeking-after" social and universal harmony through the pulsing ventricle of an ecstatic, Buddapoetic spirituality.

Certainly Pound, who Harold Oldmeadow reports, described W.B. Yeats' metaphysical ideas as "very very very bughouse," or insanely too-far-reaching, would have had a similar reaction to Kerouac, Ginsberg, and even Kandel, had he lived long enough to see Beat spirituality make its full bloom (Oldmeadow 29). Indeed, Pound was "more attuned to Chinese aesthetics than Hindu metaphysics," (though Yeats, like Diane di Prima, also read the more grounded, philosophical, Zen writings of D.T. Suzuki) and his cantos "exhibit strong Oriental influences derived from his study and translation of Chinese poetry and philosophy" (29). Following in the footsteps of Asian American scholar Ernest Fennellosa, Pound "also became entranced by the expressive possibilities of the pictographic Chinese script, charmingly describing his own idiosyncratic exploitation of Chinese characters" as "listening to incense" (29). According to Pound, Oldmeadow reminds us, the early Chinese poets were, "a treasury to which the next centuries may look for as great stimulus as the Renaissance had the Greeks," and it's hard to disprove Pound's prophecy given the degree to which Beat writers like di Prima and Kandel immersed themselves in Buddhist aesthetics and Eastern thought at large (29). "The first step of a renaissance, or awakening," Pound proclaimed, sounding a bit here like Kerouac a half century later, "is the importation of models for painting, sculpture, writing" (29). "The last century discovered the Middle Ages," Pound confirmed, and "It is possible that this century may find a new Greece in China," he subsequently hypothesized (qtd. in Oldmeadow 29-30). In spite of the degree to which Pound's own absorption of Asian literature had successfully manifested itself in his work (one critic, Richard Eugene Smith claimed that Pound's own version of the minimalist haiku paled in comparison to the great Matsuo Basho's), Pound's imprint, like Whitman's, can be seen as a stream flowing vibrantly into the sea of Beat Buddhist poetics.

Furthermore, like Emerson, and Thoreau, Pound recognized the impact Whitman had—and would come to have—when, in his poem "A Pact," featured in *Poems from Lustra: 1913-15*, Pound apostrophically tells Walt Whitman:

> I make a pact with you, Walt Whitman -
> I have detested you long enough.
> I come to you as a grown child
> Who has had a pig-headed father;
> I am old enough now to make friends.
> It was you that broke the new wood,
> Now is a time for carving.
> We have one sap and one root -
> Let there be commerce between us.

Here, in this pivotal lyric moment in American literary history,

Pound figures himself not a Wordsworthian "child" who is an imaginative "father to the man," but is instead a "grown child" who has at last succumbed to the sprawl of his father's shadow. However, despite the fact that the poem's speaker comes kicking and screaming all the way to the wide chamber door of his "pigheaded," self-reliant, insatiably verbose and spiritually over-exuberant father, his willingness to "break wood" here with his literary-spiritual ancestor, signifies a kind of a "carved-out" communion between two poets across half a century of time and a great chasm of aesthetic space. It is this poetic "commerce" that Pound shares with Whitman—a veritable poetic truce between the father of American-poetic, cosmic-consciousness, and the eventual father of American-poetic, aesthetic-minimalism—that we eventually see embodied by the Beats of the 1940s, '50s and '60s.

More specifically, while the Beats certainly adopted Whitman's own hybrid spirituality informed by Hindu mysticism and Buddhist creed, they simultaneously embraced, with a good degree of vigor, the ideas Pound mapped out for a new aesthetic geography in his "Imagist Manifesto." As Smith reminds us, in his Introduction to *America Zen: A Gathering of Poets*:

> The principles of Imagism as expressed in the "Imagist Manifesto" include "the use of the language of common speech...the exact word, not the nearly-exact, not the merely decorative word," free verse cadences and freedom of subject matter with an emphasis on the concrete. Imagist poets shared these goals: "To present an image. We are not a school of painters, but we believe

that poetry should render particulars exactly and not deal in vague generalities" and "To produce a poetry that is hard and clear, never blurred and indefinite." Ultimately, they [the Imagists] declared *concentration* as "the very essence of poetry." Recall that these poets were breaking from the rigidity of the 19th century formalism and lofty Romanticism. Though Emerson, Thoreau, and Walt Whitman were calling for [their own] new concreteness, the predominant 19th century voices were still Henry Wadsworth Longfellow, John Greenleaf Whittier and Edgar Allan Poe. (11)

The employment of "common speech," the use of the "exact word," the elimination of unnecessarily ornate or "decorative" language, the "rendering" of "particularized" vision through an exacting diction and a tightly-compressed, poetic line, and a poetry "hard" and "clear" and full of deep "concentration" characterized the poetry of Pound, H.D., and the Imagists. And it was to this poetry that Diane di Prima was exposed when she entered Swarthmore College as a sixteen-year-old in 1951. There, at Swarthmore, di Prima began immersing herself in the canon of "modern masters," which included some of Pound's writings on the importance of "making" poetry "new." In fact, when asked to comment on her literary influences, di Prima, after speaking for a while about Keats and, before that, about important Zen teachers and writers, goes on to tell Tony Moffett in *Breaking the Rule of Cool*:

> I went to Swarthmore for a year and a half and they had all these modern poets. In college, I found Auden on the shelf there in the bookstore, and then I found Pound. And everybody had a charge account at the bookstore in those days. I left college after a year and a half because it wasn't suiting my desire to write. And just before I left I hit the bookstore and I charged—oh, you know, *The Cantos*, *Spirit of Romance*, *Make it New*, and cummings, and Eliot, of course. But the main thing that happened to me was I left college when I was eighteen. I started at sixteen and I went home to my little apartment on the Lower East Side, and I began to read everything Pound suggested in *The ABC of Reading*, which meant I found a Homeric Greek grammar....A little Dante, [too] you know. Language became an obsession. And by '55, I was writing to Pound and I went to visit him for two weeks in St. Elizabeth's [Hospital in Washington D.C.]. He was staying with his close friend, Sheri Martinelli, the painter, kind of you could say his mistress, but he was in the hospital and she wasn't. (Grace and Johnson 93)

Based on her encounters with Auden, Pound, H.D., Eliot, and (as we will see in the following chapter) the Zen essays of D.T. Suzuki, in the 1950s, it is clear that di Prima, at a very young age, was learning that poetry could in fact "make nothing happen." It is poetry, with its sensory-spiritual intelligence which allows one to make silence speak, or make death sing, as we shall see later in di Prima's apostrophic poems to her children and her Zen teachers.

What's more, it was in these early years that di Prima took on Pound as her own aesthetic teacher beyond the college doors, embodying a kind of artistic, Emersonian/Poundian/Troubadourian/Zen Mystic self-reliance, first in 1950s Manhattan, and then, in the subsequent decade, in San Francisco. By studying Pound as closely as she did, "reading everything" he "suggested," di Prima gained access not to "part of a world," but a "whole" in which Confucian thought and Chinese and Japanese aesthetic sensibilities "entwined" with "Homeric" and Sapphic Greek, and even Italian Dantean and Petrarchan, linguistic textures upon the creative canvas of a page. Surely, in the weeks in which di Prima corresponded with Pound and then visited him (as Whitman had, wounded civil war veterans) in the hospital in D.C., di Prima must have felt herself becoming absorbed by a rich spiritopoesis emanating from both directions, east and west. With the gates of poetry opening, she must have heard, at least upon the page, Pound speaking the following lines from "Ortus," as if directly to her:

> Surely you are bound and entwined,
> You are mingled with the elements unborn;
> I have loved a stream and a shadow.
> I beseech you enter your life.
> I beseech you learn to say 'I'
> When I question you;
> For you are no part, but a whole,
> No portion, but a being. (9-16)

Here, in the concluding stanzas of the short, but elegantly

compact "Ortus" (which first appeared in the magazine, *Poetry*, in April of 1913), Pound, sounding perhaps more like Whitman than usual, is awakening both the reader, and the poem's addressee, to the potentiality of her own interdependent and "mingled" humanity, emphasizing a theme prominent both in Western poetry (via Donne, Wordsworth, Whitman) and Asian spirituality (by way of the *Dhammapada* and the *Tao Te Ching*). "Ortus," meaning "sunrise" in Latin, presents a view of the world in which a broad, luminous sun is rising over the self, calling the individual consciousness into being, awakening the poetic, and at least semi-autonomous "I" from the depths of "shadow." "Ortus," which can also mean "risen," "appeared," "originated," or "sprung" (depending on its feminine or neuter, first or second declension) is a poem about the self "springing" into being as it rises to meet a world that has previously manifested itself as an apparition to the eye/I. Whereas in his "Station of the Metro," which was featured along with "Ortus" and "A Pact" in the aforementioned April 1913 issue of *Poetry*, depicts a Parisian-metro station in which apparitional faces in a "crowd," manifest themselves to the poet-observer as half-shadowy "petals" on a "wet, black bough," the world presented in "Ortus" presents a word in which a "window" opens beyond "shadow" onto a stream of fuller awareness.

Thus, Pound, like Zen teacher Shunryu Suzuki, was one of the people who exposed di Prima to this literary world enlightened by poetry and its immense attentiveness to particulars—both within the environ of the poem, and within the very natural world from which the lumber of language is carved. We can thus curiously imagine, or gently assume, that Pound, who died before di Prima released her own Pound-inflected volume of poems, *This Kind of Bird Flies Backwards*, would have appreciated the first of di Prima's "Three Laments," which reads:

> Alas
> I believe
> I might have become
> a great writer
> but
> the chairs
> in the library
> were too hard. (1-8)

Here, a poem without punctuation floats within the compressed space of its Poundian lineation, but its tone, reminiscent of Pound's often gritty, curt diction, (as seen in "The Pact") seems to almost punctuate itself. In a mood of Poundian, playfully-prodding, Zen-neoclassicism, the speaker renders herself as the Wordsworthian, Whitmanesque, anti-scholar whose study "out of doors" (recall Wordsworth "quitting his books" in "The Tables Turned") will advance her poetic craftsmanship more than it will her potential for being a "great writer." Preferring the smoother, more fluid world of nature, where the universe "mingles" and is "entwined," di Prima takes a Poundian, Snyderian Zen axe to the library's "hard," wooden chairs and heads for the woods, knowing full well, as she makes her way for Concord, or the mountains north of San Francisco, that she might have to peacefully settle, like her fellow female Zen-Troubadour, Lenore Kandel, for the role of "Awakened Singer Outside the Library Doors."

Out into the Exalted Open, and through the Meditation Hall Doors: Shunryu Suzuki Roshi, Diane di Prima, Lenore Kandel and a "New Knowledge of Reality"

In the final poem of his 1954 *Collected Poems* titled "Not Ideas About The Thing But the Thing Itself," a Wallace Stevens, who had been immersing himself in Chinese Landscape painting, Zhaoming Qian reveals, speaks the following lines into post-atomic America like an oracle prefiguring the dawn of a new age:

> It was not from the vast ventriloquism
> Of sleep's faded papier mâché . . .
> The sun was coming from outside.
>
> That scrawny cry—it was
> A chorister whose c preceded the choir.
> It was part of the colossal sun,
>
> Surrounded by its choral rings,
> Still far away. It was like
> A new knowledge of reality. (9-18)

Here, in lines that shimmer with the sound of something "new," "spun in the sun," to recall Lawrence Ferlinghetti's "diamond," "lotus," "Confessional" from earlier in this chapter, a Wallace Stevens who had just recently received "two large scroll paintings" (one Chinese, one Japanese) from his friend, the Korean Buddhist poet, Peter H. Lee, is hearing the "far away" music of a "new" and "colossal" "reality" playing harmoniously on the Hartford horizon, in the melodic key of "c." Evident in the poem's layered and pressed, linguistic, "papier-mâché diction", is the "colossal" impression those scrolls no doubt made on Stevens, reigniting within him "an old passion" for Far Eastern philosophy, poetry, and art (Qian 164). However, even without the "gifts" from his poet-friend, Lee, Qian notes, "Stevens' meditative creativity was to shine in his final phase," a phase in which, as he had early on in his Zen-inflected poetic career, Stevens saw, dare we say "heard," the "sun coming from outside" America. Like Pound, he was "listening to incense," or, in Stevens' case—with a marked double entendre— hearing the "choral" "ring[s]" of a new planetary awareness, a new spiritopoetic song.

Some 3,000 miles from Hartford Park, Stevens was hearing the subtle clamor of a gently-composed, but still rapturous, melody beginning to harmonize in San Francisco's Haight Asbury and North Beach. In a sense, we might even see Stevens' "Not Ideas About The Thing But the Thing Itself" as Modernism's last literary frontier, with Stevens recording its last sunrise here in the wistful, but still ecstatic final, papier-mâché pages of his "colossal" poetic notebook. Seen in this light, the poem mourns the end of an epoch in which there could be, as Williams and Pound both insisted, "no ideas but in things" concrete, no faith in grandiose, philosophical, or spiritual generalization, and no blurred or "blunted" language, to recall Larry Smith's discussion of Pound's "Imagist Manifesto." From another angle, though, we might read Steven's last collected poem rather as a "bridge" between Modernism and Beat Generation, Post-Modern spiritually-hybridized aesthetics. Seen from this alternate promontory, Stevens' "prophecy"—if it's just to call it that—resembles more an exciting possibility, an innuendo of a "new consciousness" projected in the singular voice of the winged "chorister" whose melodious c-note "precedes the choir" of birds that trail it as it rises up over the sun-speckled, eastern horizon, sailing over the clouds toward hemispheres unvisited.

Whether Stevens was aware of it or not, his vision of a harmonious "chorister" carrying a "new knowledge" or spiritopoetic awareness of "reality" was less "far away" than supposed. Though Stevens, like Yeats, di Prima, Ginsberg, Kerouac, or even Kandel, was ostensibly familiar with the widely popular writings of the Japanese philosopher, D.T. Suzuki, (as Qian claims in his article on "Late Stevens, the Orient and Nothingness"), there is no way Stevens' could have (at least consciously) predicted the arrival of the charismatic, compassionate Zen "chorister" and spiritual teacher, Shunryu Suzuki Roshi, in San Francisco on May 23, 1959 (Qian 166). In San Francisco, Shunryu Suzuki came to represent for a community of Buddhist aspirants and Zen poets like Diane di Prima and Lenore Kandel, what Pound, in some senses, came to represent for Modernist poets decades earlier. Unlike Pound though, who was no spiritual guru, to say the least, Suzuki Roshi was a teacher who was available, who was "on the spot," as it were providing spiritual guidance and a certain poetic brand of spiritual insight that brought sometimes overly-exuberant Beat writers "down-to-earth." Summing up Suzuki's impact on the community of writers, artists, Beatniks, and visionaries that comprised the Haight-Ashbury scene between 1959 and 1971, Harry

Oldmeadow explains that Suzuki, "an obscure and humble Soto [Zen] monk" originally arrived in San Francisco to "serve the Japanese, American congregation at the Soto Temple Sokoji," but when he first landed on American soil, there was "little to indicate that Suzuki would "become one of the most influential of the many remarkable Zen roshis who came west" (293). During his time in San Francisco, Suzuki built, from the ground up, both the San Francisco Zen Center, (which di Prima, Kandel, Ginsberg, Snyder, and others all visited) and the Zen Mountain Center at Tasajara, (which di Prima visited, both with Kandel, and, later, with her children, on a family retreat), "taught a generation of Westerners who were to carry American Zen into the twenty-first century," and wrote a "quiet and modest book" titled *Zen Mind, Beginner's Mind*, which was "widely successful in capturing many readers hitherto utterly ignorant of Zen" (294). With this list of accomplishments in full view, it is fair to say that Suzuki had more than a verse to contribute to the song that Zen poets, practitioners, painters, and musicians were collectively composing in 1960s San Francisco.

Another source of Suzuki's popularity among Beat poets may have stemmed from the fact that, during WWII in Japan, the Roshi had become "conspicuous by his refusal to help the governments inspire the populous with the proper samurai spirit" (Fields 228). Instead of conforming to the Japanese government's nationalistic, propagandistic agenda of providing Japanese soldiers with a superficial "course in zazen before being sent off to the front," Suzuki formed an intimate discussion group that conversed about the "implications of militarism" for sentient beings (228). Like the Beat poets, who were more politically active and socially conscious than either their Modernist relatives or their Transcendentalist ancestors, Suzuki felt that war was an inherent crime against the human spirit and an injustice to all species, human and natural, inhabiting the earth. Suzuki's deep concerns for humanity, his suggestions for the most effective practices of meditation, and his ideas about creativity and the imagination can be found in the aforementioned *Zen Mind, Beginner's Mind*, which featured recorded lectures Suzuki delivered in San Francisco between the years of 1959 and 1971. It is in these lectures he gave some of the most crucial, practical, and inspirational advice to San Francisco Beat poets of the sixties (as we shall see in the subsequent chapter on Suzuki's direct influence on the life and poetry of Diane di Prima). But at the root of all Suzuki's teachings, what really drew the Beats toward Suzuki as a spiritual teacher and creative muse was his belief that, at its core, "Zen Mind," was the practice of "Beginner's mind" (Baker xiv). What moved poets like di Prima and Kandel, was Suzuki's tireless commitment to a practice rooted in "the innocence of the first inquiry—who am I?" (xiv). Moreover, "the mind of the beginner is empty, free of the habits of the expert, ready to accept, to doubt, and open to all the possibilities. It is this kind of mind which can see things as they are, which step by step and in a flash can realize the nature of everything" (xiv). Both at the Zen Center, and in their own private meditations, di Prima and Kandel were experiencing "flashes" of Buddha "nature" in their beginning minds, and they were recording "everything" they witnessed or imagined in the pages of a poetic present unfolding before their awakened eyes.

Thus, with Zen "beginner's minds" full of literary and spiritual enthusiasm, but devoid of rigid preconceived notions of what art ought to be in post-war America, Diane di Prima and Lenore Kandel arrived in San Francisco in the 1960s "free of the habits of the expert" poet while also carrying with them volumes of canonized, metered verse. Much to their creative advantage, di Prima and Kandel arrived in the city by the bay at precisely the moment in which, as Kerouac had suggested, a new spiritual awakening was taking place, something brand new "spun in the sun," Ferlinghetti concurred. Sitting as they did, at the Zen Centers in the city and in the mountains of Northern California, these female poets from the boroughs of Brooklyn and Manhattan found in Suzuki Roshi a "down-to-earth" Japanese spiritual teacher who provided them with enough personal and spiritual grounding (tale-bone literally pressed down into the zazen cushion) to explore the far limits of their Buddhist spiritopoetic visions. This combination of direct, first-hand, authentic Zen meditation, combined with a sprawling and sometimes unwieldy aesthetic, spiritual pluralism (simultaneously merging with their deep literary awareness of Poundian, Chinese attention to "particulars" and a spontaneous, Whitmanesque, Indian, "cosmic consciousness") served to produce some of the most authentic lyric poetry of the second half of the American twentieth century. As Oldmeadow confirms, "The poetic atmosphere of this new generation" of poets in San Francisco was "eclectic, visionary, polytheistic, ecstatic, and defiantly devotional" (248). In San Francisco, di Prima and Kandel produced a "defiantly" ritual poetry of religiopoetic freedom that, through the primary vessel of tactful, modest, and egoless Zen Buddhism, allowed them to pay homage, dream after, and devote themselves to a wide cosmos of muses, heroes, gods, and goddesses that included "American Indians, Shiva, Krishna, Buddha, Thor...Saint Francis" and even the very astrological signs themselves (248).

More specifically, with the guidance of Shunryu Suzuki Roshi's simple, but potent Zen aesthetic of an "ego burned all the way through," Diane di Prima and Lenore Kandel ironically produced a more honest, subjective, lyric-Buddhist-poetics where an excessively self-conscious "little-mind" preoccupied with its own autonomy moves out of the way in favor of a vast, limitless, infinitely-connected "big mind" where a poem becomes not a place of self-worship, but rather a means to invite the world in. Stated another way, a uniquely selfless, Buddhist poetics, allowed each of these female lyric poets an opportunity to sit with themselves and meditate on what "selfhood" might in fact mean to them in an age when the cultivation of atomic warfare and excess of materialism made it increasingly difficult to see oneself amid the not so pristine political and social mire. If Jonathan Culler is correct in his Hegel-inspired assessment that the lyric poet is indeed someone who "absorbs into himself [or herself] and stamps it [the world] with inner consciousness," and that "the unity of the poem is provided by this subjectivity," then indeed Kandel and di Prima were, without question, lyricists of the first rate (2). Yet, it is critical that, in the case of these "American Buddhist Poets," that we use a word like "stamped" with a degree of delicacy, or caution. While assuredly Beat Generation writers were imprinting their own pronounced, "subjective," artistic visions of a "new consciousness" on the pages of American letters, the word "stamp" here is perhaps a bit strong, for it fails to recognize the way in which the universe, itself an author of an indelible, kaleidoscopic cosmic poetics, is writing these poets' lives into the tapestry of language, divinity and being.

With that small, but important distinction in view, this book does in fact align itself with Culler's simple, yet revelatory claim that "the goal of reading a lyric is to produce a new interpretation"—or, as Stevens would have it—a "new knowledge" of lyric-poetry. For in his introductory chapter of *Theory of the Lyric*, Culler suggests that for a long time in the "academic world," critics have been interpreting lyric poetry as a "representation of a subjective experience" in which the "lyric is spoken by a persona, whose situation and motivation one needs to reconstruct" (2). A bit further on in his discussion, Culler expands upon this long-accepted mode of lyric interpretation by asserting that while indeed "many great poems in the English tradition are dramatic monologues" or "fictional imitation[s] or representation[s] of real-world speech act[s]," this "model" of reading lyric poetry as a work of fiction with a central dramatic actor or "character" often "deflects attention away from what is most singular or most mind-blowing even, in those lyrics, and puts readers on a prosaic, novelizing track" (Culler 2). Culler's interpretive distinction between a "prosaic track" and a lyric track" is significant to a reimagining of the creative possibilities that American lyric poetry might offer, and allows us to recognize the ways in which a "novelistic" approach to American Buddhist poetry is in fact a limiting, if not misguided interpretive method. Because the Buddhist American poems of Kandel and di Prima often feature poetic speakers who dart elusively and egolessly around the imagined space of the poem, a standard, "dramatic" reading of their Beat Buddhist poetry will often fail to catch the nuances and spiritopoetic resonances that emanate from their work.

Furthermore, Culler's revelation that contemporary poetry "lack[s] an adequate theory of the lyric" gives credence to a project such as this one, where the hope is to explore and expose new methods for seeing, hearing, interpreting, imagining, and internalizing the vast echoes of contemporary American poetry. In the pages that follow, I hope to present a uniquely resonant "East-West Poetics" of vitally-imagined, already-constructed, experiential lyric space that resembles a fully-realized, literary event which can take on diverse meaning without relying on what Culler terms "prosaic reconstruction." Hence, in this book, I want to stretch and make elastic the boundaries of a lyric poetry aptly written and imagined at the very margin of American poetic consciousness between the years of 1959 and 1972. While, a book applies certain close-textual reading and formalistic strategies that allow us to consider the way interpreters of lyric poetry might for instance "praise, imitate, translate, memorize, evaluate or identify allusions or rhetorical strategies" a poet might employ, I want to suggest, through this literary historical, spiritopoetic project, that lyric poetry can also be seen as a conversation within, throughout, over, and across time (5). Moreover, a Buddhist lyric poetics such as the one exhibited by di Prima and Kandel, serves the very function of opening the mind to the doors of what a spiritually-engaged lyric poetry might make possible beyond the boundaries of conventional modes of theorizing about and meditating upon twentieth century poetry. With the somewhat unanticipated flourish of American Buddhist criticism and theory in this early segment of the twenty-first century—and rapid increase of globalization in this epoch—it is a ripe moment for an examination of the Beat Generation's Buddhist poetic tendencies, precisely because these Beats, some fifty to sixty years ago, were already theorizing about ways to reimagine the language(s) we use, the poems we write, and the globalized, multi-ethnic lives we have ultimately come to live.

This book thus not only aligns itself with Jonathan Culler's contention that lyric poetry "involves a tension between ritualistic and [potentially] fictional elements," his suggestion that we ought to begin considering lyric poetry as a "performance or representation of the "character of an event," but it also aligns itself more broadly with Rick Fields', Gary Storhoff's, and John Whalen Bridge's conception of American literary history as a fluid narrative illuminating the porous interconnections between a host of vibrant imagined literary communities. In the first part of this book, I explore the way in which, within the imagined literary community of San Francisco, poet Diane di Prima formed a very "real" bond with Zen teacher Shunryu Suzuki Roshi, one that allowed her to conceive of poetry as a kind of Zen "ritual" chant in which one draws a potentially mournful, bewildering and suffering past into a Zen, present-tense, here-and-now, which allows her to strive toward actualizing the Buddha's vision of the cessation (or at least the quelling) of suffering. In her Suzuki-inspired, Zen, Beat poetry, di Prima carves a way through suffering and opens a space for joy and communal healing and selfless-self-realization through the vessel of a sensory engagement with the world that awakens both poet and reader to the very paradoxical fact of a pain-tinged, yet ecstatic human existence. Like her Beat sister, di Prima, Lenore Kandel enacts a Zen-sensory "performance" which presents a lyric poem not merely as a well-wrought urn to be investigated and dissected for meaning, but instead as a kind of spontaneously-emerging lotus-consciousness unfolding in leaves and petals of infinitely strewn poetic potentiality.

However, whereas in di Prima's poetry, *Zen* Buddhism forms the core and subsequent encasing of her lyric, spiritual exploration, for Kandel, Zen Buddhism is rather a springboard for a spiritopoetic leap into a diffused poetic consciousness, a consciousness in turn *suffused* with Tantric Buddhist, Tibetan Buddhist, and even Indian mystical awareness. Through the use, then, of poems, interviews, Zen aesthetic statements, Zen lectures, Eastern visual imagery, literary criticism, literary historical commentary, and a small underground newspaper, I will try and illuminate the numerous ways in which a Zen Buddhist spiritual aesthetic dynamically manifested itself within the lyric poems of Diane di Prima and Lenore Kandel, two uniquely Beat "Blue-Light Dakinis" who have helped guide American poetry, and readers of American poetry, beyond seemingly impermeable political, spiritual, and artistic boundaries, toward a new geography of poetic consciousness.

PART ONE

Spirit from Sense

Diane di Prima's Zen Broth Simmering

Introduction: Diane di Prima, Buddhist Image-Making, and the Taste of a New Consciousness

With his spirit floating through her room, Diane di Prima wrote the following poem for her Zen teacher, Shunryu Suzuki, following his death in 1971:

> after you died, I dreamed you were at my apartment
> we ate Soba together, you giggled and slurped at it
>
> you said "Don't tell them I'm not dead"
> & pointed down the street toward the Zen Center
> "I don't want them to bother me"
> we laughed and drank the broth.
>
> I kept that promise: I think they still don't know.
> <div align=right>(<i>The Wisdom Anthology…</i>)</div>

This sparsely punctuated, minimalistic poem, titled "For Suzuki Roshi," dedicated to her teacher of almost a decade, not only expresses an intimacy and a candor uniquely characteristic of di Prima's Buddhist poetry, but also encapsulates the impact that studying and practicing Buddhism, as well as living in San Francisco, had on Diane di Prima's poetry and her life. For di Prima, her engagement with Zen Buddhism—and perhaps more importantly, her many hours meditating with Shunryu Suzuki Roshi—proved to be a key ingredient in her development as a Buddhist-Beat poet of the 1960s.

In fact, during that decade, Buddhism—and Zen Buddhism in particular—became the rich "broth" which di Prima, and many of her peers, drank feverishly, searching for warm sustenance in the years following WWII, and during Vietnam. Through Buddhism, the Beat poets explored what Ginsberg (in his Introduction to *The Beat Book*) called "the textures of consciousness," and Buddhism became the heat boiling a broth of diverse, unorthodox, aesthetic attitudes, controversial political perspectives, and seemingly un-American spiritual interests and affiliations (Ginsberg v). Stirring this curious "broth" of the '60s spiritual, inward-turning sensibility was Shunryu Suzuki Roshi, a leading Japanese Zen teacher at the time, and a man with whom Diane di Prima "sat" zazen in order to "know his mind" and discover what Zen Buddhism had to offer her, a young poet from the East Coast whose own sensibilities were significantly informed by 1950s New York's avant-garde (Knight 123). For di Prima, meeting "the little Suzuki" (a name Shunryu coined to humbly distinguish himself from Zen philosophical giant, D.T. Suzuki) proved to be "the first time" in her "twenty-eight years" that she "encountered another human being and felt trust" (123). "It [studying with Suzuki] blew my tough, sophisticated young-adult's mind," di Prima told fellow Buddhist Beat poet, Anne Waldman, revealing that spiritual and aesthetic "trust" are essential ingredients in the development of serious and "sophisticated" poetry (123). Indeed, Roshi's influence, both spiritually and creatively, further ignited a change taking place in the consciousness of a writer who, along with fellow poets Kerouac, Ginsberg, Snyder, and Kandel, had already been reading the Zen writings of Japanese transplant D.T. Suzuki and began studying meditation with choreographer James Waring in the 1950s (Johnson and Grace 90). Therefore, even before she traveled to the West Coast to study with Suzuki Roshi, di Prima was highly aware of the fact that, as D.T. Suzuki wrote in "A Sense of Zen," "Zen Buddhism in its essence is the art of seeing into the nature of one's own being, and it points the way from bondage to freedom" (3).

Therefore, when she traveled to the West Coast for the first time in what Timothy Gray calls "the tumultuous summer of 1961," di Prima "freed" herself, significantly, from the conventionality and "bondage" of some of the East Coast's traditional literary values and "pulled up stakes," ultimately "mov[ing] west for good" (163). Despite already living in "voluntary poverty" before she permanently moved to the Bay Area, di Prima began living even more modestly by becoming "more involved in Asian religions forbidding material attachment" (165). She began visiting Shunryu Suzuki at the San Francisco Zen Center, started engaging regularly with fellow poets and spiritual aspirants at the East-West House in San Francisco, and started attending retreats at the "new Buddhist Monastery" at Tassajara "nestled deep in the mountains," of Northern California (165). Thus, we might say that, in the 1960s, di Prima's bohemian proclivities turned from spiritual curiosities and youthful ideals into a more pronounced devotion to Zen spiritual practices and beliefs. Actually, it was in the following year, 1962, (according to numerous interviews and biographical sketches) that she initiated her deep encounter with Shunryu Suzuki Roshi's brand of graceful but direct, nurturing but disciplined study and practice of Zen Buddhism. Based on allusive remarks di Prima makes in interviews and Zen aesthetic statements, and on the very Suzukiesque tone that resonates in some of her poetry from 1962 forward, we can not only sufficiently say that di Prima studied Zen privately with Suzuki to become more spiritually adept, but also attended many of his public lectures and discussions on Zen, later transcribed in the classic book, *Zen Mind, Beginner's Mind* (1970) because she found Zen's ego-dissolving impulse and its emphasis on presentness (living in the "moment") personally and artistically inspiring. In fact, a close reading of Suzuki Roshi's lectures presented in *Zen Mind, Beginner's Mind* (particularly the talk titled "No Trace" in Part Two of the text), alongside di Prima's own comments in poems, interviews, and Zen aesthetic statements (as we will see later) yields an acute awareness of the way in which di Prima's own poetic practice, what she herself has called the "work" of non-attaching and "clearing the mind" for the "work" of "images" was significantly shaped by her immersion in Suzuki's teachings (Tonkinson 140). Reflecting on the import of Suzuki Roshi's influence on her writing, di Prima (Tonkinson reports) observes that, "by practicing [Zen Buddhism] deeply, the images start to flow. My teacher [Suzuki Roshi] never contradicted this. Dharma practice and art are two sides of the same coin" (120). Thus, we might say that Suzuki's presence manifested itself in at least two ways in di Prima's life: first, as dharma teacher and guide through meditation, and second, as poetic and philosophic muse, grounding her work by subtly, but powerfully, participating in the growth of a body of poetry rich in Buddhist imagery and spiritual sensibility.

Above all, it is her belief in poetry as a practice of "image-making" or generating connectivity between author and reader through the vehicle of unmitigated, first-hand, sensory experience that defines di Prima's work as a Beat Buddhist poet. More pointedly, poetry, for di Prima, is a sacred blend of the ethereal and the everyday. It is a labor one accomplishes *tastefully*, like the making and the drinking of "broth" in the spiritually-resonant poem for Suzuki Roshi, *tactfully*, with taste and attention to the sacred craft of poetry, the sacred act of being human, and by way of an "open-handed," *tactile* engagement with poetry, spiritual devotion, nature, and humanity at large. It is in this spirit of taste and tact—and with an emphasis on tactility and sensory awareness to experience—that I wish to present di Prima as a markedly spiritual American writer, as a Buddhist poet with a special respect for Suzuki's lucid, spontaneous, and creatively non-judgmental and compassionate craftsmanship. Additionally, and perhaps more significantly, I want to trace the way, di Prima—a Beat Buddhist poet with a special reverence (like her teacher) for the role that hands play in shaping and then transferring creative energy, global awareness, and personal illumination for/to readers, poets, and students throughout a vast and daunting universe—uses her compassionate Buddhist heart, her receptive Buddha hands, her powerful chanting voice, her luminous, clear-visioning eyes, and her egoless Zen mind to see over and beyond the boundaries of personal, cultural, and spiritual consciousness in post-WWII America. Finally, through her deeply private encounter with the process of Buddhist self-actualization and a Buddhist attempt to awaken us to the jagged, but refractive beauty of transient human existence, di Prima's poetry turns inward toward and then unfolds outward from what her contemporary Robert Creeley has called "her [own] search for human center" in order to touch the core of the Beat Generation's deep devotion to decreasing suffering through the power of poetic speech (vii).

"Benevolent Impulses:" Early di Prima, D.T. Suzuki, and a "Sense of Zen"

Before exploring in detail the impact of di Prima's Suzuki-inspired poetry of the San Francisco sixties and early seventies, it helps to understand the tenor of di Prima's less practically engaged Buddhist poetry of the late fifties and the spiritually significant, but still distant Buddhist encounters she had in the few years leading up to the publication of her first book, *This Kind of Bird Flies Backwards*, in 1958. In contrast to Ginsberg's controversial, rhapsodic political-spiritual poem "Howl" (1956) and Kerouac's questing, soul-searching *On the Road* (1957), di Prima's poems in *This Kind of Bird*, though certainly Buddhist-tinged, resemble more Pound's East-Asian minimalist efforts and H.D.'s pre-New York school, avant-garde modernism than they do Ginsberg's or Kerouac's maximalist, line-lengthening, consciousness-expanding, spontaneous poetry. Far more like taut, Modernist meditations on the nature of death, time, and the human experience of isolation, di Prima's early work exhibits the spirit of a poet who made multiple visits to St. Elizabeth's Hospital in 1955 to visit and talk poetry with an ailing Ezra Pound than it resembles a young poet who met Ginsberg and Ferlinghetti for the first time in '56 and then met Ginsberg, Kerouac, Orlovsky, and Corso in '57 (di Prima, *Pieces of a Song* 198). Indeed, the di Prima of the mid-to-late fifties was a poet just becoming aware of what "Beat" aesthetics really had to offer in terms of aesthetic experimentation, which I call "its radically egoless poetry" or "poetry of the ego beat back." Rather than being steeped in a pronounced Whitman-inflected, Beat poetic conversation that began springing up in the late forties, di Prima's early aesthetic allegiance lay more with Modernity, with Projectivism, with what Peter Puchek calls "New York School personalism" and with a Buddhism encountered in books than a thoroughly lived one—a markedly more individualized one than the shared one she would encounter a few years later living in community with Beat writers in San Francisco (234).

Nevertheless, while di Prima's early-Buddhist poetry of the late fifties is both conceptually and visually diverse from her Zen Buddhist poetry of the sixties and seventies, it would also be insufficient to say that di Prima's poetry did not resemble a terrain richly fertilized by the seedling of 1950s Buddhist zeitgeist emerging both in San Francisco, and in certain literary and philosophical circles in New York's Greenwich Village and on campus at Columbia University. For as Ellen Pearlman posits in *Nothing and Everything: The Influence of Buddhism on the Avant Garde: 1942-1962*, "[Though] D.T. Suzuki's influence was limited initially to a select number of cognoscenti who attended [his] open classes on Buddhism taught at Columbia University from 1952-1955," he was not a "household name" yet at the time and was "neither written about in popular publications nor discussed on topical TV shows," the way Kerouac, a Buddhist appropriator of sorts, or Alan Watts, a Western-Zen philosopher, had been (xi). However, by the late fifties and early sixties, this was changing. D.T. Suzuki's name became as recognizable as the titles of his widely read books on Zen. As Pearlman observes, by the end of the decade, Suzuki's teachings had "seeped into the worlds of music, painting, poetry and literature, performance, dance and intermedia" (xii). Composers like John Cage, poets Jackson MacLowe, Allen Ginsberg, Jack Kerouac,

Diane di Prima, West Coast poet Gary Snyder, (who stored, among other notable East-Asian texts, copies of Suzuki's Zen books in milk crates) along with a host of well-regarded painters, sculptors, and choreographers had caught D.T. Suzuki fever, and were well on their way to engaging in long artistic affairs with Zen through various mediums of art.

As a matter of fact, di Prima speaks directly to the influence of Suzuki's Buddhism on her early experience as an artist living in New York's Lower East Side from 1951-1961. In a retrospective interview titled "Pieces of a Song," conducted by Tony Moffett in July, 1989 (and then reprinted in Johnson and Grace's *Breaking the Rule of Cool: Interviewing Reading Women of the Beat Generation*), di Prima elaborates on the way Buddhism has influenced her career as a poet. Candidly, di Prima tells Moffett in the interview:

> ...[Y]es, I think that Buddhism in general has been an influence. But way back before any of us practiced Zen or anything really, D.T. Suzuki's books were an influence in the early fifties. And I remember because one of my early teachers in the arts was a choreographer named James Waring, and he was close friends with Merce Cunningham and John Cage and so the influence of D.T. was in a cultural lineage there. And we [Beat poets] were all reading that stuff and it was influencing us in a great number of ways in our work. I would say that some of them [artists and poets] were accepting that every form—it goes back to the notion of organic form— every form is real so you don't have to manipulate your

work to get it into shape. Or as Robert Duncan has put it, consciousness itself is shapely, so trusting the basic field of consciousness and not trying—because the writing of the late forties and early fifties was [still] very obsessed with the "well-wrought urn"....So it [Suzuki's Buddhism] was a big influence on opening the form and stepping outside of one's own consciousness. (Johnson and Grace 90)

Di Prima's words here not only reflect a poet completely "open" to discussing her poetic influences with a kind of Zen directness, but they also provide unique insight into the philosophical, spiritual, and artistic climate into which she was assimilating in her twenties in Manhattan. Further, what's initially striking about the passage is the access which di Prima provides for seeing into her aesthetic "lineage" and the cultural and artistic legacy to which she sees herself tied as an American poet of the twentieth century. And yet, equally as significant, is the way in which this word "lineage," echoes from the passage with a double resonance not only reflective of artistic legacy, but also spiritual inheritance. Historically speaking, one of the keystones of Zen Buddhism is the sacredness of its lineage and the way in which it has been passed on directly by Bodhidharma (who first brought Zen, or Chan, from India to China) forward, and from patriarch to subsequent Zen patriarch living to transmit Zen to the next generation of practitioners. So what di Prima means then, when she says "legacy," is the sacred "transmission" (a word she uses frequently) of spiritual and artistic energy from person to person, from individual hand to individual human hand. Intriguingly, Zen

Buddhist history, much like twentieth century American poetic history, is as much the story of individual enlightenment as it is the collective, communal transmission of experience, insight, knowledge, wisdom, and practice, from person to person and group to group, across months, years and decades of time, giving added texture to di Prima's commentary.

Tellingly, di Prima's sense of the importance in receiving spiritual and artistic influence first-hand here echoes a comment she made in a talk delivered at Naropa University in Colorado (which she co-founded with Allen Ginsberg and Anne Waldman in 1974). In this talk titled, "By Any Means Necessary," reprinted in the anthology *Beats at Naropa*, di Prima, discussing her experience running various small presses and the importance of publishing something one can "hold" in one's "hand," emphatically says the following to students and teachers at Naropa: "Think about broadsides and little magazines—what you have then—you have something in hand, in your hand….It's something you're doing by hand—with your hands—and infusing with energy to pass onto other people" (Waldman 197). What di Prima seeks to relay here to students and peers in her Naropa talk closely resembles what she relays to Tony Moffett in her 1989 interview. For di Prima, poetry begins at the level of the body, and crosses the body's threshold when the artist transfers and transmits the body's spiritually-charged energy through the medium of touch—touching pen, page, word, and the hands of others. This kind of direct contact which di Prima endorses is the catalyst for becoming aware of a wider "field of consciousness" that lies beyond the page, beyond touch, taste, smell, sight, and sound. While some readers less familiar with Buddhism's intricacies may hold the belief that Buddhism champions a negation of sensory experience, this is incorrect, because in Buddhism, sensory experience plays a valuable role in human understanding, and consciousness itself is considered to be a "sixth sense." Di Prima, a long-time practitioner of Zen, and later Tibetan Buddhism, is aware that sensory connectivity with the universe, between its natural and human species, is indeed the first level of awareness, the doorway out of the darkness of self-centeredness and a lack of intimacy with a world collectively inhabited. Di Prima's allusion to the poetic theories of Robert Duncan, a figure associated with the Beat and Black Mountain Schools, and with the San Francisco Renaissance that took place in the fifties and progressed through the sixties, is an important one because it exemplifies multiple "lineages" from which di Prima has received direct poetic inspiration. New York School, Black Mountain School, Beat Generation, Avant-Garde Art, Imagism, Zen Buddhism, Tibetan Buddhism, Hinduism, Catholicism, various Native American Traditions, Greek/Pagan Mythologies, Feminist discourse, and Schopenhauer's philosophy (which she read at age twelve) are the many lineages that inform di Prima's work. However, in di Prima's early work it is the specific transmission of spiritual and creative energy she received from reading D.T. Suzuki and following the precepts of Duncan's poetry as an "open field" in which the poet places increasing trust in the "shape" of his or her own awareness that most deeply infuse themselves in di Prima's work in *This Kind of Bird Flies Backwards*, which she published before moving to San Francisco.

Flights of Compassion: di Prima's Early Buddhist Sensibilities in her "Songs for Baby-O"

Di Prima's unique Buddhist awareness of the dolor and suffering with which humans enter and exit the sentient world is on display in two early poems in *This Kind of Bird Flies Backwards*. The first of these poems, titled "Requiem," which appears on page 14 of di Prima's *Pieces of a Song: Selected Poems*, speaks almost directly to the Zen notion that "we are finite," "earth-created" beings who "cannot live out of Time and Space" (Suzuki, "The Sense of Zen" 17). The poem, which utilizes the figurative device of apostrophe (as does the poem "For Suzuki Roshi") to create intimacy between the poem's speaker and the deceased child she is addressing, is made of 27 taut, compressed lines that exude a mournful tenderness reminiscent of imagist poems like Williams' "Widow's Lament in Springtime" and Pound's "The River Merchant's Wife." But di Prima's "Requiem" song for "Baby-O" does contain more of the subjective emotion of a lyric poem; it is more a minimalist blues elegy than an intellectual treatment of death in verse. With a kind of Zen directness and a spiritual intimacy, the speaker of the poem's opening stanzas, imagining Baby-O's inevitable discomfort in death, admits:

> I think
> you'll find
> a coffin
> not so good
> Baby-O.

> They wrap you in
> Pretty tight
>
> I hear
> it's cold
> and worms and things
> are there for selfish reasons. (1-11)

Di Prima's willingness to address directly the finite reality of transient human existence here is a hallmark of her Buddhist poetry. In these small compressed lines, small as the child in the "cold" worm- and death-inhabited "coffin," the poem's speaker attempts to bring warmth to the deceased child's spirit through a tone of intimacy and a language of genuine benevolence and maternal concern. Though di Prima makes no direct reference to reading D.T. Suzuki's essay "The Sense of Zen" in her interview with Tony Moffett from July, 1989, her "sense" of Zen and what it has to offer poetry in its attempt to address Buddhism's first noble truth that life is comprised of infinite suffering resonates strongly with what Suzuki has written in that essay. Powerfully, in an earnest manner attractive to poets of the fifties who had grown skeptical of salvationism and theories of the afterlife, Suzuki, in the 1949 essay, posits that "Instead of allowing the body to grow moldy, 'wither' away...the object of Zen is to save us from going crazy..... This is what I mean by freedom, giving free play to all the creative and benevolent impulses inherently lying in our hearts" (3). Suzuki's rhetoric here is a markedly inward-turning one, a pronouncedly compassionate one with special emphasis on the individual's capacity for reducing suffering in the world around him or her. The "benevolent impulses" of which Suzuki speaks here are representative of the potential we have for utilizing the "creative" powers that each of us has "lying inherently in our hearts."

Seen in this light, di Prima's "Requiem" can be seen not as a funeral poem defending the speaker's need for a proper Christian burial, but instead a Zen-Buddhist song for a child whose premature passing does not change the real and finite fact of death. To do anything other than provide genuine comfort and concern for the child would be to stoop to the level of the worms that "selfishly" invade the casket to feed on the defenseless human body. It is therefore with great human dignity, a deeply compassionate heart, and a powerful, but measured tone, that di Prima delivers the poem's final stanzas. With special attention, then, to the child's physical positioning within the tight confines of the casket, the speaker tells the deceased:

> I think
> you'll want
> to turn
> onto your side
> your hair
> won't like
> to stay in place
> forever
> and your hands
> won't like it
> crossed
> like that

> I think
> your lips
> won't like it
> by themselves. (12-27)

Though it would be physically impossible for the child to heed the advice given to her, di Prima's attention to physical detail, body positioning, and sensory experience here conveys an honest audiovisual picture of the kinds of thoughts that pass through a parent's mind after the death of a child. In simple, curt mono-, di-, and trisyllabic words, the speaker allows us to almost feel a body moving around inside a coffin and moving to turn "on its side" in an effort to gain more space; however, because this act, for the dead, is an impossible one, the "turn" onto one "side" is more a turn of the mind, or, as it were, the speaker's mind turning over upon itself within a room of deep concern. More specifically, it is the speaker's own mind which resembles a coffin of worry in which thoughts and concerns for Baby-O flow interminably within a box of mental preoccupations. The short, non-extended lines of the poem, with their short-breathed, almost breathless formation, represent a speaker who struggles to move within the confines of the poem's own dying body, a poem moving like the small child toward its final moment.

This fact that both the infant's body and the speaker's voice are enclosed within "forms"—the infant's body within the "tight" casket, and the poet's voice and speech within the poem's taut rectangularity (a kind of box of death she has made with the lumber of language)—seems to work almost antagonistically against the radiant sincerity and almost playful childishness of the speaker's tone at moments in the poem. For it is in lines 16-19, when the speaker tells the deceased child, "your hair / won't like / to stay in place / forever," she sounds perhaps most like a young girl herself, playing with the child's hair as if before a long mirror in her memory. But no real mirror here exists for the speaker of di Prima's poem, as she brushes through a deeper kind of mourning—the sorrow a parent encounters upon losing a child. Writing here, within the great poetic tradition of poems which have addressed the theme of infant death, as Ben Johnson has in "On My First Son," and as di Prima's contemporary, Donald Hall, has in "My Son, My Executioner," her poem, like theirs, is more than a meditation on passing life; it is, more specifically, poetry's attempt to eternalize human life without arresting or stopping the flow of its energy. For di Prima, a Buddhist poet, knows all too well, that "hair," "won't like / to stay in place forever," because all things, continue to have motion, continue to fall, tussle, topple, slide, and change directions. All of life is characterized by motion that persists even in our wake. Not even "hair" untouched by the human hand will remain static, fixed in one place "forever."

"Requiem," is, then, in a certain sense, a poem elegizing the death of an idea; it holds a funeral, as it were, in which a speaker concerned for the well-being of a deceased child, shows little remorse for the static notion of a "forever" in which things cease moving, in which the human body becomes static after the soul leaves its corporeal frame. Indeed, the final lines of "Requiem" point toward a poet raising serious concerns about human life after death. Di Prima contextualizes her concerns, however, not within a sky-signifying heaven to which all souls inevitably ascend, but instead, situates her meditation on the buried body of "Baby-O" within the context of a Buddhist consecrated ground, a ground to which Buddha pointed to in the moments preceding enlightenment. In those moments preceding his spiritual awakening, when the Buddha faced the temptations of Mara, it was the ground that he claimed would testify on his behalf; it was the earth that he would call to witness his liberation from suffering. Therefore, when di Prima says to the dead child who is both there and not there, "and your hands / won't like it / crossed / like that," it is with a fear that "crossed" hands will constrict her posture and prevent her from experiencing physical liberation that she utters the lines. With special emphasis once again on "hands," which, for di Prima, like the Buddha, represent openness of spirit, human connectivity, transmission of dharma, and connectivity with the ground (and the natural world) the speaker surmises here near the poem's end that the child won't like spending an "eternity" here in the posture that is socially acceptable and culturally expected of the dead in the west. Here, the word "crossed" resembles the word "cross," which signifies both a religious symbol at which the poet is raising a brow and a ritual way in which the child's death continues to "cross" the poet's consciousness. Finally, the word "crosses" not only reflects back upon the word "forever" by way of a shared assonant "e," evoking a delicate near-rhyme figuration, but it also folds back to touch its Christian-resonant counterpart "forever" by way of standing equally alone on its own line within the poem. Here, di Prima is drawing particular attention to words with religious meaning in the poem for the precise purpose of contrasting them with her own simple, non-symbolic, and direct Zen diction at other moments in the poem. Thus, we can say that the poem relies on a special friction, a unique dynamism catalyzed by the collision between the values of her own Italian-Catholic heritage and her immersion in Zen reading and study, namely the works of D.T. Suzuki, and the Zen interests held by various teachers she studied choreography and poetry with throughout the fifties.

No segment of the poem, however, more directly speaks to Suzuki's notion that Zen unearths from an individual the "benevolent impulses lying inherently in our hearts," than does the poem's final stanza (3). At last, when di Prima's speaker, earnestly, but also quite surprisingly says, in perfect iambic-pentameter cadence enjambed over four lines, "I think / your lips / won't like it / by themselves," the poem's final stanza marks a leap in poetic affect and heightened empathy on the part of the speaker. It is in this final stanza where the poem's speaker becomes more emphatically maternal. It is, moreover, at this precise moment in the poem, where the speaker's previously potent, but measured voice, her Zen-unattached, selfless, intimate concern for the child become more an indication of her own desire for the child's love than for the child's simple well-being. For it is into the subtext of this final sentiment that the poet's own desire for the child's kiss projects itself. However, in spite of the fact that, at first glance, this might suggest the encroachment of the speaker's own ego upon the selfless landscape of the poem, the poem's conclusion is more a confirmation of a love that wells up in the speaker spontaneously through the process of writing the poem than it is an imposition upon the poem's restraint, the child's own (posthumous) desires, or the dignity of the child's death. The poem is more an enactment of the sudden leap which Zen Buddhists call "satori" than it is the poet's slip of the ego or "hand." Contrarily, what we witness is di Prima's delicate treatment of death here, as well as her speaker's "benevolence" toward, and compassion for, the child who, here at the poem's end, has become "mother to the woman," to turn a phrase from Wordsworth. In many ways, it is the child who has taught the elder how to write and live more tenderly, how to experience the art of losing more profoundly. And yet, were it not for the speaker's deep sensory concerns—her profound care for the infant's hands, hair, and lips—the leap in consciousness toward the realm of pure love would not be possible.

If the poem "Requiem" is indicative of di Prima's early "benevolent" Buddhist impulses then the poem "For Baby-O, Unborn," which appears on page 17 of *Pieces of a Song* reflects an even more pronounced and compassionate Buddhist concern for human suffering. Once again writing in the apostrophic mode, di Prima addresses the same "Baby-O" she casts as the central figure of "Requiem," but here, with increased sensitivity and unparalleled honesty, di Prima writes:

> Sweetheart
> when you break thru
> you'll find
> a poet here
> not quite what one would choose.
> I can't promise
> you'll never go hungry
> or that you won't be sad
> on this gutted
> breaking
> globe

> but I can show you
> baby
> enough to love
> to break your heart
> forever.

In these sixteen tender, "breaking" lines, in this poem "gutted" of excess language and sentiment, we can see and hear di Prima's Zen aesthetic trajectory, years before she traveled to San Francisco and began practicing Zen meditation. Here, the body of this thin poem itself is like an "electric battery" with a "mysterious power" that stimulates the reader's capacity for empathy and deep feeling (to recall D.T. Suzuki's "Sense of Zen"). This speaker's empathetic, compassionate temperament "breaks thru" in the poem's inciting lines when she shows a capacity to imagine the way in which "Sweetheart," Baby-O, might conceive of a life with a mother whose vocation affords her little luxury or comfort. Of special importance in the poem's first stanza is the phrase "break thru," which serves the double role of capturing not only the physical act of childbirth, but also the child's breaking through and into the realm of consciousness and human awareness. As mentioned earlier, it is through the vessel of sensory description that di Prima evokes an awareness of a deeper realization—that the child's birth is not only the beginning of Baby-O's self-awareness, but also of her mother's own new consciousness. The mother's/speaker's consciousness in the poem now includes her child's emerging perception of her mother, which is indicated in lines 3-5, when the speaker reveals that her child will "find / a poet here / not exactly what one would choose." The child's birth thus incites a significant recognition for the poem's speaker, a moment when the speaker is able to conceive of herself as she really is—a poor poet with little to offer a young child in the way of security. The poem's opening stanza is therefore indicative of a moment of pronounced Buddhist self-awareness in di Prima's poetic corpus where, stepping outside herself and assuming the child's perspective, di Prima's female speaker is able to conceive of herself neither as poet nor activist. In the end, with increased humility, she conceives of herself principally as mother, as an every-woman toiling along with other sentient beings on this "gutted" human globe.

It is, not coincidentally, at the heart of the poem, in its pivotal and transitional second stanza, where the speaker admits that she can't "promise" the child food or happiness, that the poem's subtle, but profoundly Buddhist tones rise to the text's surface. For it is in this stanza where the poet's Buddhist belief in the notions that suffering exists and that desire is the cause of suffering, emerge. For instead of deluding Baby-O, (minimizing delusion is paramount for Buddhists) the speaker admits outright that there is nothing she can promise the young child that will diminish the inherent suffering that exists within the world's "globe." Additionally, the poet's vivid description of the world as a "gutted," "breaking," "globe" not only emphasizes the dynamism and activity with which di Prima imbues objects and forms within her poetry, but also reflects back on a kind of intensely visual and tactile language manifested in the "Requiem" poem for Baby-O discussed earlier. Here, the word "gutted," which evokes both the gutted mother's belly after birth, and the gutted body of a ravaged creature, mirrors di Prima's squalid image of "worms" di Prima employs in "Requiem" in order to evoke the decomposition of the human body over time. Coupled with that image, the alliteratively rendered image here of the "gutted globe" takes on another sensory and conceptual register, one reminiscent of Shakespearean language employed in tragedies like *Hamlet* and *Macbeth*, both of which can be seen as profound meditations on human mortality and the endurance of the human spirit after the body's dissipation. Could we read this pair of apostrophic poems to Baby-O as di Prima's own dramatic/dharmic workings-out of the relationship between body and spirit, life and death? Is this a place in di Prima's poetry where her eastern and western sensibilities merge in interesting ways to address questions fundamental to the very fractured, "breaking" core of our fragile human existence?

Whether or not the poem's pronounced but inconsistent employment of iambic meter is enough to offer a direct answer to questions of the sort, there is indeed a sense in the poem of a poet drawing on all the raw materials available to her in order to address the question of whether or not art should provide recompense or uncompromising truth in the face of suffering and inevitable mortality. It is with emphasis on the visual and the tactile—"but I can show you"— that di Prima's speaker seems to offer an answer to that seemingly unanswerable question. As if drawing back a veil (Buddhism's veil of "maya," or illusion?), the light touch of di Prima's poetic hand, coupled with the compassionate tenor of her voice, reaches out to the child (and to the reader) at poem's end when she tells Baby-O that she can show her "enough to love" and "break her heart / forever" (13-16). In surprising fashion, instead of telling the child that she can show her child "enough love," the poem's speaker tells the young girl that she can show her "enough *to* love"—

75

enough worth loving—in the world she will come to inhabit. This small addition of the preposition "to" in the poem's thirteenth line is of paramount significance, and I would argue is one of the smallest, but most significant turns of phrase in di Prima's early poetry. For this slight turn outward suggested by the preposition "to" is the hallmark of a linguistically and spiritually mindful poet who, instead of placing emphasis on an assumption that her own love can save her child from sadness or hunger, it is precisely, and only, the "gutted," flawed, imperfect world in all of its tragic beauty which will make life truly worth living, persisting through, and loving in return. It is poetry, art, and the sacred which the speaker can show her daughter in order to make her recognize that life is indeed full of beauty in spite of the fact that it is "gutted" by malevolence, corruption, greed, ignorance, and, at times, an absence of compassion. Seen in this light, having a broken "heart" can be conceived of as positive by the speaker at the poem's end. To live with a broken heart is to live tenderly and with a crack that "forever" exposes one's interior world to a pain that is fundamentally human. Unlike the word "forever" which resonates with a kind of static impossibility in the poem "Requiem," the word "forever," here at the end of "Song for Baby-O, Unborn," resonates with a sweet and dolorous continuity, an infinite trust in the spontaneous trajectory of life's painfully, but dynamically interconnected web of beauty, pain, suffering, and compassion. Seen in this light, Song for Baby-O, Unborn," can be seen as an even more Zen poem than its counterpart, "Requiem," and reveals a development in di Prima's early sensibilities, even within the very same volume of poetry.

"Leaving No Trace": Shunryu Suzuki, the 60s, and di Prima's Poetics of the Burning Ego

Having now examined the way di Prima's early encounter with Buddhism in the 1950s formally and thematically informed her early poetic sensibilities, we can more fully begin to explore the degree to which she engaged Buddhism as an art and a practice in the 1960s. However, we need to continue to see and hear her poetry in the context of her own reflections and insights on her spiritual engagements in order to elucidate the degree of direct contact di Prima was making with Zen during the years she spent in San Francisco. In the same interview with Tony Moffett from July, 1989, di Prima not only discusses the extent of D.T. Suzuki's early influence on her thinking, but also reveals the influence Shunryu Suzuki Roshi had on her as a young poet and budding Buddhist practitioner throughout the 1960s. About Suzuki Roshi, di Prima tells Moffett:

> And then, in the early sixties, I met Shunryu Suzuki, who became my teacher and started the Zen Center in San Francisco.... I studied with Shunryu Suzuki and started to sit Zazen around '62 and moved out to San Francisco in '67, and one of the main reasons was to sit at Zen Center there and study with him..... After he died, I didn't stay with Zen Center because organizations per se are not my thing, and there wasn't that feeling of strong pull to the lineage heir of Suzuki who was an American man [Richard Baker], but I continued to sit and I would

use various teachers who had been at Zen Center all the time: Katagiri Roshi, who taught in Minneapolis, and Kobun Chino Roshi. (91)

While the above passage, at first glance, appears to serve more as a historical or chronological time-line for tracing di Prima's practical engagement with Buddhism in the 1960s, the short passage from this interview, more significantly, illuminates the degree to which Buddhism was much more than a bohemian "fad" for di Prima. Quite the opposite, di Prima's spiritual experience, rather than a broad immersion in eastern religion was marked by a very intimate desire to make more personal and more intimate contact with Zen by way of Suzuki Roshi's transmission of the dharma. Additionally, it is not only di Prima's interest in studying with an authentic Japanese Zen teacher which stands out as a signifier of her own artistic authenticity and her reverence for her teacher's own *Japanese* Buddhism, but it is also di Prima's lack of interest in studying Zen with an American teacher (Shunryu Suzuki's heir, Richard Baker) which reveals her own pronounced reticence about studying what we might call a "Buddhism twice-removed." Though di Prima herself did not study and practice Zen in Japan like fellow Beat poets Gary Snyder and Philip Whalen, and though she did not study and practice indigenous forms of Buddhism and Hinduism abroad as Allen Ginsberg did when he traveled to India in the last sixties and early seventies, di Prima's remarks here are more widely reflective of the Beat poets' insistence on receiving direct spiritual transmission from Eastern teachers like Shunryu Suzuki, Katagiri Roshi, and Chogyan Trungpa—the latter who accepted di Prima as his student of Tibetan Buddhism in 1983 when she decided she needed a spiritual practice that contained more "magical elements" to infuse in her poetry—di Prima tells Moffett in "Pieces of a Song" (91).

Two decades before di Prima would begin studying the magical elements of Vajra Buddhism with Trungpa at Naropa, and almost a decade before the death of Zen teacher, Shunryu Suzuki, di Prima indeed received a direct transmission of the dharma so pervasive in its nature that its very luminosity and insistence on self-awakening and personal truth deeply permeated her poetry of the sixties and seventies (and beyond). Primed by a growing "sense of Zen" which she began cultivating by reading D.T. Suzuki and studying with James Waring in fifties New York, di Prima arrived in San Francisco with an eager "beginner's mind," a mind open to all that Suzuki Roshi had to offer in the way of axiomatic language and deep faith in the power of meditation. Interestingly, in a 2014 interview with Jonah Raskin for the *San Francisco Gate*, di Prima, when asked what artistic "success" meant to her, quickly and directly alluded to something her teacher, Suzuki Roshi, told her in the 1960s. In typical pin-point, razor-edged diction, di Prima tells Raskin:

> My first meditation teacher, Suzuki Roshi, a Zen Buddhist, told me, when you burn, burn completely so you leave no trace behind. I'm not attached to any particular result. My mantras are "keep making art" and "if you make a big mistake, forgive yourself." I don't try to make anything into something other than what it is. The world is perfect as it is. You are perfect as you are, though you have to get back to work to re-activate the perfection.

This segment of the interview with Raskin offers a crucial glimpse into the core of Diane di Prima's spiritual and aesthetic sensibilities. Her recollection of Suzuki's insistence on "burning completely" and "leaving no trace" is indicative of a poet who completely embraced Zen Buddhism's beliefs in egolessness and selflessness. To "burn completely" is to utilize all of the intellectual, spiritual, and creative energy which has been bequeathed to us as human beings, and then to infuse that energy throughout our art. To withhold this energy is to think and act selfishly, even ignorantly. Art, for di Prima, is an act through which one gives all of oneself, genuinely and authentically. So, to "leave no trace" is to leave no residue of the ego in the mind's wake. To "keep making art," then, serves as defense against the ego's desire to leave its "traces" of vanity and its need for self-affirmation. As di Prima says in the title of her aforementioned Naropa lecture, we must keep making art for others "by any means necessary." There is therefore, in di Prima's view, a kind of fire always burning, at least faintly, below the artist's consciousness. Art needs to continue simmering, like a good "broth." Art never stops boiling and radiating its light, much the way a teacher's memory continues to warm the drafty rooms of poetic memory. Thus, to "burn completely," to manifest the full radiance of one's potential, be it artistic or spiritual, requires letting go of the self that clings to its creation and wishes to impose its illusion of permanence upon a poem or work of art. Additionally, to "forgive" oneself for "mistakes" made, as di Prima suggests in the interview, is to acknowledge the fluidity of life, the perpetual flux of thought within the human mind (what Shunryu Suzuki called "the little mind," in order to distinguish it from "big mind" or vast, universal mind). For di Prima, a crucial part of living and being an artist is to admit that the mind is flawed and prone to error. To accept the error of one's ways is therefore to awaken to the inherent futility of one's own existence, and to accept that we are "perfect" precisely because we are transient beings who "burn" to an end, not artists playing god upon blank slates eternal. We can continually "reactivate" our fluid and energetic "perfection[s]" by simply continuing to do the work of knowing, the work of being humble, creative, and self-aware, as di Prima does throughout her Buddhist non-fictive prose and her Zen poetry.

Furthermore, the passage from the 2014 interview from the *San Francisco Gate* is significant not only in the way it displays di Prima's complete embrace of what Zen has to offer her aesthetic project, but it also serves the distinct purpose of establishing deeper connectivity between di Prima and Suzuki Roshi—between di Prima's poetry and Suzuki's poetic lectures delivered in San Francisco throughout the 1960s. More specifically, the Zen axiom to which di Prima alludes in the interview with Raskin points directly to one of the lectures from Suzuki's *Zen Mind, Beginner's Mind*, titled "No Trace," where Suzuki discusses with Zen students and adopts the imagistic and compelling notion of "burning completely" so as to "leave no trace" of past experience upon the plane of the mind. Though we have no evidence telling us that di Prima visited the Zen Center on the very night Suzuki originally delivered the talk that came to be titled "No Trace," we can deduce, from her specific allusion to Suzuki's language in the interview with Raskin, that she and Suzuki Roshi indeed discussed the concept of "No Trace" on other occasions, and that the concept was impactful enough for her to mention it some fifty years later in her interview with the *Gate*. Textually speaking, "No Trace," appears about a third of the way through Suzuki's book, and is, in my estimation, the pivotal chapter in the second section of *Zen Mind*, titled "Right Action." In the chapter, Suzuki expounds upon the way we humans develop certain fixed, "preconceived notions" that "shadow" us and stifle us, mentally and spiritually, causing us to perpetually continue attaching ourselves to past actions which in a sense become the source of further illusion. Our proclivity toward being attached to certain thoughts, Suzuki seems to say, (like thinking of past artistic "successes" as permanent, enduring, or final, for instance) not only "leaves some trace or shadow" on the individual mind, but also "gives us many other [false] notions about activities and things" (Suzuki 47-48). "These traces and notions make our minds very complicated…," Suzuki goes on to say, and they originate in the "relative mind," the mind that seeks always to relate present experience to past experiences, to versions of prior experience which seem to resemble, and then gradually over-shadow, present reality, but are in fact definitively not unconditioned reality in the present (48). The mind's "traces" are, in essence, shadows which obscure our experience of presentness and cause us to live always somewhere else, in terms of something or someone else.

A bit further on in "No Trace," we encounter in Suzuki's talk some "traces" of quintessential Zen language quite reminiscent of di Prima's own words in the *San Francisco Gate*, words which di Prima seemed to adopt as her own spiritual and artistic mantra. "If you attach to the idea of what you have done," Suzuki posits, "you are involved in selfish ideas" and "limit the actual experience you might have right now" (48). Though it is indeed important to "remember what we have done," Suzuki admits, clinging to past actions, past triumphs, past successes has a way of making our dynamic lives static. "So, in order to not leave any traces" when we do something, we should do it with our "whole body and mind" and do it "completely, like a good bon-fire" (49). By burning completely, both the Zen practitioner and the poet practitioner can receive the light of awareness, the clear-mindedness and open-heartedness necessary to having an intimate relationship with the world "at hand," the world that is right within reach. Therefore, according to Suzuki (and his student di Prima), "Zen activity is activity that is completely burned out, with nothing remaining but ashes" and "the secret of this activity is transferred from Buddha to us" (50). The dynamic process of allowing traces of past thought to pass without attachment across the surface of our consciousness is fundamental to what Zen offered Diane di Prima and the San Francisco poetry scene at large throughout the fifties, sixties, and early seventies. Because poetry itself is quintessentially a process of "transferring" creative energy, as di Prima often reminds us, flowing line by line, across and down the page, from writer to reader, the Zen belief in "burning completely" through to the bottom of a thought, action, or page of artistic consciousness without leaving "traces" of excess thought, figures itself as the appropriate metaphor for American poetry of the mid-twentieth century looking to burn off all traces of mainstream consumer rhetoric, military propagandism and conservative ideology. We can see, consequently, how the precise economy of Suzuki's Zen language would appeal to poets like Ginsberg, Kandel, and di Prima, poets who moved west in order to craft a poetry that spoke more to the dynamic, primordial, illuminated, raw, and quintessential experience of being human in a century "shadowed" by American cultural hegemony and traced by fears of political and spiritual unorthodoxy. The Beat poets moved west hoping not to be shadowed by "preconceived notions" of what art or life might be. They moved to San Francisco, instead, to "burn all the way through" personal and national delusions of grandeur, in order to discover what art and life indeed *were* at the spirit level.

Ego Burned to Ash: Sensory Awareness and the Path to Zen Connectivity and Personal Illumination in "I Fail as Dharma Teacher" and "Tassajara Early 1970s"

For the Beat Buddhist, di Prima, the process of conquering ego and mastering the self by "leaving no traces" of "preconceived notions" of reality based on past "successes" becomes a prominent theme in her more overtly Buddhist poetry in the years during after her meditations with Suzuki Roshi, from 1962-1970. Even if it requires admitting her own inability to transmit the "Dharma"—the teachings of the Buddha—as she does in the poem "I fail as Dharma Teacher," di Prima reveals a willingness to falter as teacher-poet-practitioner so long as communal enlightenment emerges as a result of her own personal, spiritual, or pedagogical shortcomings. Therefore, with the selflessness of a bodhisattva, someone Allen Hunt Badiner in *Dharma Gaia* defines as a "living being who experiences the spirit of enlightenment" but "vows to help all beings manifest their own awakening" (241) di Prima, in "I Fail as Dharma Teacher," confesses:

> I don't imagine I'll manage to express Sunyata
> in a way that all my students will know & love
> or present the 4 Noble Truths so they look delicious
> and tempting as Easter candy...
> present the Eightfold Path like the ultimate roadmap
> at all the gas stations in samsara
> But, oh, my lamas, do I want to
> how I want to!
> just to see your eyes shine in this Kaliyuga
> stars going out around us like birthday candles
> your Empty Clear Luminous and Unobstructed
> Rainbow Bodies
> swimming in and through us like transparent fish.
> (1-4, 12-20)

Here, di Prima's poetry rises, "Clear" and "Unobstructed" to the transparent surface of all that Buddhism has to offer the poet and the world she compassionately, egolessly inhabits. "I Fail as Dharma Teacher" confirms that "wisdom" indeed lies in "insecurity," as the title of western Buddhist Alan Watts' well-known book suggests. The poem radically but also level-headedly proposes that Buddhism's dharma does not exclude "failure" from its geography of truth, its topography of self-knowing. Furthermore, like her teacher, Suzuki Roshi, di Prima is aware of the way that the "little mind" in all of its false assumptions about absolute truth and its attachment to past experience can inhibit a teacher's (or Zen student's) capacity to experience sudden awareness and deeper connectivity with the world. Moreover, "I Fail as Dharma Teacher" paradoxically reflects di Prima's attempt to allow "failure" to serve as an agent in the realization of a vast, "big mind" and all of the expansive spiritual, intellectual, and creative possibilities it manifests for Buddhists.

Additionally, as Suzuki does quite often in his writings, di Prima appears to suggest in the poem, that attainment of an ultimate or final truth in the form of nirvana is predicated not so much on the practice of perfect religious faith or incessant spiritual devotion, but more so on an ability to recognize error as a vehicle of personal understanding and collective growth. For di Prima's students (here, her students at the Naropa Institute), and for her readers and other Buddhists reading the poem, a sincere and genuine attempt to transmit the dharma, to teach the way of the Buddha—and to admit some failure in doing so—is a kind of blessing the poem's speaker offers with earnest compassion and reverence for the process of continual self-awareness. It is di Prima's authentically self-deprecating confession of failure as teacher that ironically "teaches" us more profoundly about "Sunyata"—the "recognition that there is no permanent, unchanging element within the [individual] self, and that deeply, illumined human understanding lies less on self-affirmation than on "interbeing," "the Buddhist teaching that nothing can exist by itself," not even the seemingly perfect wisdom of the Buddha himself (Badiner 242). It is instead one's commitment, one's enthusiasm, one's "love" of a subject—of a doctrine or an art—that determines the degree to which one fulfills one's dharmic role, the manner in which one walks one's own dharmic path in the wake of Buddha. It is therefore significant that, in the poem, di Prima's concern about not presenting Buddhism "deliciously" enough to her students is proof enough that Buddhism, for the poet, is something with deep flavor, something which she knows comes with an acquired taste (to once again evoke the image of di Prima eating "Soba" noodles in a "broth," in her California apartment, with her teacher's ghost). It is di Prima's own rich taste for Buddhism's schema of the "4 Noble Truths" that she wants to serve at precisely the right temperature to her students.

Aesthetically speaking, the poem's figurative language, though principally Zen in flavor, is composed not only of Buddhist religious allusion and imagery but is also somewhat infused with a western religious rhetoric that combines to help the poet express the paradoxical notion that "failure" is something savory, rather than something bitter. Much in the way that she utilizes a Buddhist lens to engage Christianity in a more universal discourse on the complexities of human mortality in her early poems to "Baby-O," di Prima, in "I Fail as Dharma Teacher," actually employs a Catholic simile to more sweetly and tastefully convey the core teachings of Buddhism to her voracious, young students. As she admits early on in the poem, she wants the "4 Noble Truths," on suffering and the cessation of suffering, to be "as delicious / and tempting as Easter candy" to her dharma-seeking students (3-4). The youthful, innocent quality of the simile employed here not only represents another moment where the poet derives spiritual insight from sensory experience, but it also signals a moment in her Buddhist project when we hear echoes of a Roman Catholic upbringing in her work. More pointedly, as di Prima thinks about ways to more "deliciously," more tastefully present the subject of Buddhism to her students she interestingly reverts, momentarily, to her own girlhood spent with her Italian grandfather in Brooklyn, New York. Much like her early poems to

"Baby-O," di Prima's language here engages resurrection imagery visible in her employment of the word "Easter" which may be as indicative of her desire to resurrect the true spirit of Buddhism for her students—to reanimate its living presence in the modern world—as it is her own yearning to resurrect her own initial, youthful encounter with a Buddhism she first encountered in the luminous pages of D.T. Suzuki's books, and later, in Shunryu Suzuki's Zen Centers in California. Nevertheless, resurrection-tinged or not, the poem's speaker does indeed hope that her students will find the same "transmission of joy" in the dharma that she found in her life by making visits to Suzuki Roshi, and later, to Katagiri Roshi. It is not surprising then, that the poet chooses to employ the diction of a child near the end of the poem, a diction that suggests that something of a child's vision, something of a willing suspension of disbelief and a receptiveness to free play, is required in the transference of deep wisdom between people. For the reader, for the dharma student perhaps reading the poem years removed, the "transfer of energy" is felt within the snap of girlishly exuberant and unpremeditated, spontaneous words like "candy," "stars," "birthday." and "Rainbows." While, more often than not, such language would resonate with overt poetic sentimentality, it is overt sentimentality, unintellectualized language and non-judgmental Zen spontaneity of speech that di Prima is after here. Figuring herself as a child with what Suzuki Roshi called a "beginner's mind," one with clear, earnest diction, di Prima becomes a more believable woman-sage with command and Zen-like mastery over language and all of its potentially communion-obstructing pomposity and self-service. Because she is able to burn all the way through her ego, di Prima is able to serve more effectively as "Dharma Teacher" to her enlightenment seeking students.

Looking even more closely at the poem's spiritually-inflected language, we discover that the sensory words di Prima chooses in "I Fail as Dharma Teacher," not only signify her own limited autonomy as dharma teacher, but paradoxically signify the potential for spiritual awakening present in this pedagogical exchange of energy. Here in the poem's (and the classroom's) atmosphere of sensory interfusions, sight, taste, touch, sound, and smell merge in a current of impressions, a single sweep of perceptive meditation. Her students' young, vibrant "Eyes," "shining," with truth-holding, universe-lighting "stars" flickering and then "going out" like "birthday" "candles" shimmering with the fire of awakening," and students' iridescent and animated "Rainbow Bodies" swimming like glittering "fish" to the "transparent" surface of clear seeing, widened consciousness, all figure a poetry of bright, luminous vision, a poetry of "seeing into the life of things," as Wordsworth might have called it. These "lit-up" phrases gleaming from the poem's syntax further signify the poet's own "successful" internalization of Buddhism's spiritual radiance, its luminous flame. Moreover, the speaker's ability to burn through society's very limited notion of what it means to be a "teacher" allows her to recognize more lucidly her students' perfection, as they swim to the glistening surface of their own autonomous self-awareness at the poem's end.

Finally, and quite significantly, it is the poet-teacher's attention to sound—her careful employment of consonance throughout the poem—that allows the visual and tactile shared experience that takes place in this dharma class to merge and resonate most powerfully. Indeed, the most powerful of these consonant employments is the poet's use of repeating "l" sounds throughout the poem which echo with a particular lusciousness as they roll over the tongue in a savory and delicate manner. Words like "love," "look," "delicious," "fold," "ultimate," "lamas," "Kaliyuga," "candles," "Clear," and "Luminous" form a kind of music that the reader not only hears, but almost tastes within the poem's elegant synesthesia. The words themselves, almost edible, full of savory sound and audible taste, delicately "fold" together like a spiritual tapestry woven through with threads of the poet's senses. The poem's "l" sounds thus become reflective of the speaker's "love" for Buddhism and her longing to make it "Clear" and "Luminous" for her students, like a "candle" burning on enduringly into the next "Kaliyuga" or epoch of human history. The poem's reliance on the delicate consonant "l" is a phonetic signifier of the poet's recognition that future transmission of the dharma relies less on teaching it, than on a young "lama's" ability to experience its continuous luminosity and its spiritual intimacy first-hand.

Like "I Fail as Dharma Teacher," the poem "Tassajara, Early 1970s" reflects di Prima's egoless, deeply sensory, firsthand-experience with the world she inhabits as a Zen poet and Zen practitioner. However, whereas in "I Fail," the poet's unmediated human experience occurs as a result of the exchange of energy between poet-teacher and her dharma students, in "Tassajara," the sensory, spiritual interaction takes place primarily between poet/Zen practitioner and her natural environment. In this case, the environment, for di Prima, is the natural environment of the Zen monastery at Tasajara, located in the mountains of Northern California. According to David Chadwick, author of *Crooked Cucumber: The Life and Zen Teachings of Shunryu*

Suzuki, Tassajara opened its doors on a "sizzling July 3, 1967," and "150 people attended the opening ceremony" including "students and friends of Suzuki's" and the event was a "milestone in [Suzuki's] life" (281-82). Though we have no confirmation of the fact that di Prima attended the monastery's inaugural event, (after all, she was not yet Suzuki's full-time Zen student at this juncture) the Zenshinji Zen Monastery at Tassajara was for di Prima nearly as sacred a place for her as it was for her teacher. In fact, according to Chadwick, it was Tasajara that di Prima visited with her children in the summer of 1971 for a month of meditation and "family practice." During this month in the summer of 1971, Suzuki Roshi even "performed a lay ordination" for the children "telling them they were the good children of Buddha" (380). It would be sufficient to say, then, that Tassajara became a place that held deep significance both for di Prima, and for her family, friends, and fellow poets and Zen practitioners.

Though it is relatively clear that di Prima wrote "Tassajara, Early 1970s," years after she retreated to the monastery in the mountains, alone or with friends or family, it is the poem's sensory immediacy, its reverential tone, and its employment of Japanese imagery that figures the poem as one of di Prima's quintessentially Zen poems. Once again, with an ear close to the music of experience, an ear tuned to the sound of her environment, di Prima, like Basho or Wordsworth, flooded by a series of sensory recollections that fill her with presence years later, recollects in the poem's inciting stanza:

> It was the sound mostly
> the wooden han
> huge antique drum from Japan

> the stream singing over the stones
> the dinner bell
> swish of zoris
> occasional wind rattling yucca on the hill
> it was the sound & the silence
> the way the daddy long legs moved on the walls of the baths
> a string quartet
> of stringy silent legs. (1-11)

Although purely descriptive poetry is less commonly visible within the body of di Prima's poetry, within her markedly *Zen* engaged poetry, sensory imagery does indeed serve as a way of nonjudgmentally rendering experience as it really was for her, without heavy reliance on metaphor as a chief instrument of meaning-making. Therefore, here, in the first stanza of "Tassajara, Early 1970s," di Prima uses imagery and minimalism to help recreate for the reader the intensely vivid time spent on meditation retreats at Tassajara. Though she does not overtly reveal the precise "sound" that the "han" made when it was played in the monastery, di Prima's reference to its "wooden," "antique" character, allows us to hear the kind of hollow, ancient sound that the drum made for those who meditated at the monastery. Additionally, when the speaker notes that the drum is from "Japan," the reader's imagination is immediately allowed to draw its own mental picture of the monastery or zendo in which the "han" may have originally been housed. Di Prima doesn't tell us where in Japan it was housed, but instead allows us to imagine where it might have come from. We thus become involved in a collaborative process of meaning-making right away in the poem; we become "instrumental" to the poem's imaginative performance on the page, curious about the origins of the drum and the impetus for this poem's imaginative musing.

Additionally, the reference to the "han" drum also speaks to di Prima's emphasis on the role that hands continually play in creating beauty and transferring artistic and spiritual energy between people and across time. The drum, made by hand, and likely played by hand, produces a 'beat' which lingers in the listener's ear, (and the poet's own imagination) much in the way that the poet creates metric beats which linger in the ear of the reader. It is from this initial recollection of the Japanese drum that the speaker's memory also begins hearing other sounds out of the past. Therefore, when she powerfully recalls the image of "the stream singing over the stones," it is the music of Tassajara that begins to fill the room of the speaker's imagination as she speaks the poem, line by line. Here, the speaker embeds a tactile image within an auditory one. We are able to feel the stream flowing over textured stones the way we might imagine a hand moving across the face of a drum. But the stream here does not simply move down mountain over stones; it is "singing" over them, the way that poetry sings over the flow of time or the way endless thoughts move uninterrupted and unattached across the surface of a Zen meditator's consciousness. Within this uninterrupted flow of tactile, visual, and sonic recollection, impressions merge as one. Into the poet's own "stream" of imagistic consciousness the sound of the monastery's "dinner bell" breaks through, as does the onomatopoeic "swish" of "zoris" (Japanese sandals) moving across the floors of the meditation halls. The sounds are the sounds of Zen daily practice, Zen's elegant music, echoing in the speaker's memory; they are the sounds of an intimate ritual in which she participated, and as she hears them, her experience inside the walls of the monastery come flowing back to her.

In spite of the great impression that life inside the monastery made on her senses, the speaker gives us reason to believe that life outside on the monastery's sprawling, mountainous grounds was equally impactful for her. For instance, when we discover that "occasionally," a Northern California "wind" could be heard "rattling the yucca," we become quickly aware that the speaker's symphonic experience at Tassajara was also catalyzed by nature's own instrumentation, its own environmental play. Di Prima's image, while phonetically and visually pleasing here, is also an ecologically and verbally accurate one, revealing her Zen proclivity to get details just right. Her use of the verb "rattling," one we might even associate with a child playing joyfully with a toy, reflects the precise sound that wind would make as it moves through the tough, sword-like yucca plants whose leaves are grazed by the wind. There is a way, then, in which "rattling" is the best verb the writer could use here because that particular verb speaks to the singularity of the memory it recounts; the winds did not "rustle" or "graze" the yucca; it "rattled" them. Moreover, it is the participial form of the verb which reveals the way that the "rattling" has yet to cease within the speaker's continually attentive, continually present Zen mind, and her still attentive ears. The winds keep "rattling," and the poet keeps "listening." Adding to the purity of this sensory experience is the fact of the yucca's whiteness (not overtly stated by the speaker), which merges visually with the purifying image of water flowing over stones and the dinner bell's singular, perfect clang resonating throughout the onset of another evening, "silence" its own music throughout this Zen poem.

It is indeed the interplay of "sound & silence" (not one or the other, but both) that allows sensory experience to emanate boldly for the speaker years after her frequent visits to Tassajara in the 1970s. In typically Zen, non-dualistic fashion, the speaker of the poem refuses to separate sound from silence, knowing that silence is a form of sound, and that sound, inevitably, leaves an echo of silence in its immediate, or lasting, wake. The opening stanza's symphony of sound finally culminates in the speaker's quiet, but sonorous image of a "daddy long legs" that "moved on the walls of the (outdoor) baths / a string quartet / of stringy silent legs." Here, in lines increasingly whimsical, di Prima's poem resembles the more playful moments in Wallace Stevens' poetry. As noted earlier, Stevens was influenced by Chinese and Japanese art, and in his own Zen-tinged "Thirteen Ways of Looking at a Blackbird," he writes, "The blackbird whirled in the autumn winds. / It was a small part of the pantomime" (Stevens 7-8). Like Steven's blackbird whirling within the stillness of a muted landscape, di Prima's noiseless (Whitmanesque) spider is a "small part of the pantomime" that was and is her enduringly memorable and resonant experience living and meditating at Tassajara. Even in the simple act of bathing (water, too, making a quiet sound as it flows from a faucet, over a body, over stones) di Prima's attentive eye, like Stevens', takes an imagistic photograph of a minute image in the spread of the landscape and then allows the visual image to resonate profoundly through a delicate employment of sound. But the sound the spider produces, like the blackbird, is, in fact the sound of silence, which is to say, a sound beyond language. Neither the "whirling" wings of the blackbird, nor the "moving, "stringy" legs of the spider make a sound that pronounces itself to anyone but the person observing its energetic motion. Both creatures are part of poetry's "pantomime," poetry's Zen dramatization of soundless sound, its record of powerfully delicate, vastly intricate movement. Yet, it is precisely this soundlessness which reverberates like a "string quartet" within the webbing of the speaker's sonic memory. The spider's "stringy legs," consequently produce the complementary experience of "sound & silence." The poet's perceptions are both "stringy"—delicate, hair-line, and near invisible to the eye— and "stringed"—sonorous, pronounced, and audible to the ear. The speaker's sensory perceptions are complete only because they are intricately rendered, precisely because they are embedded in processes of juxtaposition and synchronicity.

Interestingly, as the poem progresses in its attentiveness to the natural music life inside and outside Tassajara, playing now more sonorously within the ear of the meditative speaker, it too (the poem) becomes more musical in its dimensions, more sonic in its response to the world's "varied carols," as Whitman would have said. More specifically, as the poem "moves" like a spider into the web of its second stanza, it takes on the very symphonic quality of the monastery from which its music has emerged. Embodying more acutely Tassajara's acoustic atmosphere, the poem's speaker, almost overwhelmed by the auricular landscape of her memory, remembers that

> It was the fish shaped bell,
> the rustle of robes, the metal disk of the gong

>   the huge bell like a bowl, the songs of frogs
>   the occasional car grinding softly to a stop
>   on the gravel of the parking lot
>   the thud of footsteps over the wooden bridge. (12-17)

    Here, in the second stanza of the poem, the landscape's powerful influence on the poet's ear is highly audible. As she gradually remembers Tassajara more vividly, her speaker's language becomes more intense, more rhapsodic, as it moves toward duplicate and triplicate registers of sound. For instance, the consonance in the phrase "fish shaped," whose "sh" sound seems to carry with it an inherent hush, prefigures the alliterative "rustle of robes," which also mirrors the wind's "rattling" of the yucca in stanza one. Additionally, a kind of cascade of consonant sounds occurs in lines two and three where words with hard endings come to dominate the speaker's language. Words like "disk," "gong," "hang," "songs," and "frogs" stand in auditory mirrors before one another as the poem's speaker strives to evoke the orchestra of quick, curt, clangs of sounds that strike her memory now, years later. Perhaps the most striking of the images in this stanza is that of a "bell like a bowl," which creates not only a sonic impression in the reader's ear by way of its use of consonant "l" sounds, but also appeals to the reader's senses of touch (the bowl's wooden texture, the bell's metal texture), taste (the rice or noodles a monastery bowl might hold), and sight (a brown bowl juxtaposed against a silver bell). Furthermore, the sounds employed here in stanza two work to gather and enjoin sounds evoked in stanza one, "stringing" them together in an auditory tapestry of traditional, Japanese-Zen imagery. The grating, rasping verbs "grinding" and "rustling" allow the "rattling" from stanza one to gain a higher register of sound and meaning, and the wooden "bowl" and the "footsteps" from wooden "zoris" on the "wooden bridge" echo the sound created by the "wooden han" in stanza one. We begin to almost hear a world of hands, feet, and wind tapping and knocking on wood, intensifying for the reader the natural quality of the experience the speaker had while at Tassajara. Therefore, just as in "I Fail as Dharma Teacher," sound seems to intensify and accumulate as di Prima's speaker becomes more deeply and more emphatically immersed in her environment. As awareness increases for the failing dharma teacher or for the reflective Zen poet-practitioner, so does the power of her listening and the force of her singing voice. Her voice becomes a bell ringing with continual vivacity, a "stream singing over the stones" of buried time.

 It is the power of the human voice, poetry's melodious power, its capacity to touch with sound the core of past human experience that indeed becomes the central focus of the poem's third stanza. Like Wordsworth walking through Tintern Abbey, singing his lyric voice into the corridors of elapsed time following his sister's death, di Prima's Zen-Romantic speaker remembers, with a voice of celebration and lament, longing and compassion, how

> It was the echoes of the voices already gone
> they hung on the air.
> Suzuki watching the rocks "so they wd grow"
> Trungpa & his young wife talking in the garden
> the thump of huge mallets making mochi
> in a hollowed-out tree stump
> to the rhythm of Japanese & American folk songs
> on New Year's Eve. (18-25)

Here, in the poem's penultimate stanza, sight, sound, touch, taste, and even smell merge in "air" as the speaker attempts to convey the mixture of joy and lament that rises up in her memory of Tassajara in the early 1970s. Though echoes of the voices of beloved teachers and friends return to her here like "folk songs" she once knew well, the echoes of the voices that hang "on the air" around her memory are indeed the voices of people "already gone." One of these gone is the voice of Suzuki Roshi, the poet's Zen teacher, who passed away in 1971. In a way, then, the third stanza of the poem is a kind of elegy for the world Shunryu Suzuki created at Tassajara, the kind of world which made it possible for poets, artists, and meditators alike to retreat to when they needed to rediscover both the beauty of nature and the sacredness of their own inner lives. The Suzuki who watched the rocks "so they would grow" is therefore not only presented in the poem as a Zen Master devoting deep attention even to what some would consider "inanimate life," but is also rendered here as a man who watched his students "grow" strong like rock and firm as stone through mediation and spiritual awareness. Interestingly, if we read this image of Suzuki watching rocks grow alongside the image of "the stream singing over the stones" in the poem's fourth line, it can be said that Suzuki's spirit, immortalized in the poet's memory, flows eternal over the rocks and stones of elapsed time. Though Suzuki, the influential Zen teacher, died in 1971, the poem seems to suggest, as di Prima's aforementioned poem "For Suzuki Roshi" does, that the death of a body is only temporary because the spirit of the teacher returns ad infinitum to the student over "the wooden bridge" of an art that can last "forever," if one approaches one's art with humility and reverence. Even her memory of "Trungpa," who would become the poet's teacher in the 1980s, "talking with his young wife" continues to flourish in the "garden" of the speaker's memory, the image of the garden here folding back to touch the image of rocks that grow when they are watered by human vision and compassion. Here, in the poet's memory, that garden chatter carries on, "thumps" on, like the drum-like patter of "mallets making mochi" for a Buddhist New Year's celebration. At last, the poet's alliterative rendering of the mallets in hands pounding glutinous rice in a "hollowed out" (wooden) "stump" prefigures her auditory recollection of the "rhythm" of "Japanese and American folk songs" picked and plucked on "stringy" guitars bellowing out of the Northern California night.

Thus, while the speaker herself may, to some degree, feel "hollowed-out" by the loss of her teacher, Suzuki, and by the realization that she may never be able to experience Tassajara (or perhaps even Zen) in quite the same way again, it is the sound, "mostly," and its accompanying silence, which serves as recompense for time rendered mute by the passing of years. It is absence, paradoxically, the very "silence" that has filled her life, which has allowed her to recognize the immense presence, the powerful music that continues filling her poetry, and her life. It is consequently in the poem's final stanza where her recognition of the transience of human life and the impermanence of shared human experience turns instead to a belief that indeed poetry, community, and the sacred may be enough to quell the human tendency to resist inevitable mortality. With a quiet, but strong, Zen-like conviction, the speaker finally says:

> It was the chanting that rose & fell like waves from the Zendo
> Crickets among the lanterns that outlined the paths

> It was the small silver bell that changed you awake
> in the dark & the young monk running by as he rang it
> & the slivers of sound small stars made sliding home
>
> as you walked to the morning zendo thru tatters of
> night sky. (26-31)

It is, ultimately, the practice of Zen in all of its ritual significance, its quieter beauty, that the speaker returns in the poem's culminating sestet, though the space between the poem's penultimate and final lines might be read as two separate stanzas of thought and attention. Here, at poem's end, it is the Buddhist ritual of "chanting" at morning to prepare the mind for meditation that floods the speaker's memory like a series of rising and falling "waves." In a sense, it might therefore be said that "chant" is the rhythm and sonic character that the poem takes on, its catalogue of sensory perceptions and imagistic incantations rising up from the page in trance-like melody. For the chant is as much the poet's own chant, as much the meditators' collective, harmonious chant from inside the "Zendo," as it is the crickets' chant buzzing up synchronously out of the corridors of grass, their creatural voices as much a source of luminosity as the very "lanterns" that "outlined" Tassajara's spiritual "paths." In addition to the voices of crickets and meditators, the poet recalls that the sound of the "small silver bell" that rang after a meditation session ceased, also contributed to the choir of mountain sounds. But when the speaker recalls that the bell's sound "changed" her "awake," she not only literally means that the bell woke meditators from deep trance, from deep visualization and deep breathing, but also that the unique sounds of Tassajara had the capacity to "change" one's life, to "awaken" them like Buddha (whose name literally means awakened one). Reminiscent, to a certain extent, of the famous final line of Rilke's "Archaic Torso of Apollo," where the poet ends the poem with the line, "You must change your life," di Prima seems to suggest that one of the ways to change one's life is to listen deeply to the power of its music so it can "change you awake." Like Buddha, the speaker of the poem is aware that enlightenment can be attained if one is willing to do the work of sitting for a long time within the earth's hold, within its deeply rhythmic throes.

Nowhere though in the poem are we more in its rhythmic throes, in its heart of its sonic cadence, than in its penultimate line when the speaker sibilantly recalls "slivers of sound small stars made sliding home." At no point in the text is the poet's attention to her environment, to the potentialities of her own vocal range, greater than in this masterful line. Here the word "slivers" circles back to touch the "silver" of the bell two lines earlier, reminiscent of a rhyme in James Wright's own masterfully auditory poem, "Trying to Pray," in which he employs a slant-rhyme using the words "leaves" and "loaves" to evoke an image of women's hands. Indeed, one must have listened a long time to the sounds the night makes, must have sat a long time in quiet contemplation to have cultivated these phonetic "slivers of sound." Thus, when the "stars slide home" at the end of the poem, there is a sense in which not only the poet, not only memory, but also language itself has "returned home to itself," to invoke a famous Zen axiom. If studying Zen is indeed a way to come "home to oneself," (as di Prima has mentioned in other of her poems) then seeing, listening, touching, and living more intimately and more acutely beside and within one's surroundings are certainly ways to come home to the earth, to come home to Zen itself. With the luminous stars above sliding energetically and then nestling into their cosmic places at the poem's end, there is a sense in which things are, at last, exactly where they ought to be, even though memory keeps them necessarily at a distance from the poet's near vision or close reach. As the poem's last line (cast off on its own to signify the transition from night to morning) echoes out of silence, it is the endless new beginning of "morning" which dawns upon the speaker, and upon the reader of the poem. By writing the poem, by listening in, once again to the music of the past, the poet has left the darkness of night behind her in tatters. Tassajara returns to her like sunlight through memory, ringing its Zen bell again in her awakened imagination.

Zen Life after Suzuki: Katagiri Roshi and Poetry's "Tangible Gift in the Hand"

As di Prima tells us in her interview with Moffett, after Suzuki Roshi's passing in 1971, she did continue meditating and listening to the sound of Zen's "silver bell" by visiting other teachers. One of these teachers was Katagiri Roshi, who frequently visited the San Francisco Zen Center in the 1960s and lived and taught in Minneapolis, Minnesota in the 1970s. Though there is little in the way of evidence detailing what di Prima felt and thought about Katagiri Roshi, her largely autobiographical poem "Visit to Katagiri," is evidence enough of the valuable role that Katagiri played in di Prima's life after the death of their shared friend, Shunryu Suzuki Roshi, in 1971. Though more similar in style to "I Fail as Dharma Teacher," "Visit to Katagiri Roshi" resembles "Tassajara, Early 1970s" in its tone of gratitude for the ways in which Buddhism has allowed di Prima to "return home to herself" time and again and to continually remember that life is a "gift" not to be taken for granted throughout the course of one's temporary life. Additionally, "Visit to Katagiri Roshi" reveals di Prima's willingness to explore, through sensory experience, through the work of making images, the limits and potentialities of what meditation has to offer a person whose principal vocation is poetry, not religious practice. Here, then, in the poem's first stanza, with relaxed diction and loose form, the poet capaciously invites us into the tenuous spaces of authorial consciousness and spiritual devotion when the speaker of the poem, recording her visit to Katagiri, admits:

> I try to tell him (to tell someone)
> what my life is like:
> the hungry people, the trying
>   to sit zazen in morsels…
> "Pray to the Bodhisattvas" sez
>   Katagiri Roshi.
> I tell him
> that sometimes, traveling, I am
> too restless to sit still, wiggle &
>   itch. "Sit
> only ten minutes, five minutes
> at a time" he sez—first time
> it has occurred to me that this
> wd be OK. (4-17)

The opening stanza of "Visits to Katagiri Roshi" reveals with a refreshing honesty di Prima's concern over the inadequacy of her own Buddhist practice, her own inability to sit "zazen" and meditate for long stretches of uninterrupted time. But it is ironically di Prima's ability to admit the error of her ways (as she does in "I Fail as Dharma Teacher") and to confess the inconsistency of her meditative practice that affirms her commitment to Zen Buddhism. Indeed, as the Buddha himself has said, in the eighteenth section of Maitreya's translation of the *Dhammapada*, "It is easy to see the flaws of others, / Hard to see one's own" (70). Certainly, di Prima's willingness to explore the error of her own ways, to "see" the "flaws" in her practice, allows us to enter the poem in a way that would not be possible without the poet's own humility and self-scrutiny. Therefore, di Prima's employment of sensory detail in the opening stanza of the poem serves to illustrate the modest, but significant, spiritual progress that becomes possible when one is aware of the power of the minute, evident in Katagiri's insistence that she meditate in "morsels" or small increments of time. As we have seen in di Prima's other Zen poems, she uses a culinary analogy to convey the true spirit of Zen. Like the "Soba" soaked in "broth" in her "Poem for Suzuki Roshi," and the "Easter candy" in "I Fail as Dharma Teacher," the morsels of Zen figure Buddhism as savory faith, a kind of spiritual delicacy that one can consume a little at a time, in sacred little ways. Zen, like Catholicism, involves an act of communion, a kind of sharing of bread (or "Soba") between teacher and student which signifies the body's coming to terms with its own human limitations. Consequently, even though the human body is prone to "wiggle," "itch," and grow restless during meditation, there is a way in which the savored exchange between teacher, Katagiri, or Suzuki, and student, di Prima, serves as an agent in spiritual concentration. Through the help of her teachers, di Prima develops a taste—a deep appreciation—for the power of sitting "zazen" for smaller periods of time because even those small "morsels" of deep concentration can provide what Wordsworth called "food for future years."

In addition to the ritual communion that emerges as a theme in "Visit to Katagiri"—and in previous poems, as well—di Prima's audible struggle with meditative practice allows us to consider her poetry as a practice or performance of openness where, according to Zen poet and practitioner, Ray McNiece, "poet, poem, and listener, merge interdependently as satori" (19). Indeed, in di Prima's "Visit," the writer, the writer's words, and the text's various listeners—the attentive Zen Master, Katagiri Roshi, the poem's various readers, and the poet's own conscious and unconscious selves— form a kind of sangha or spiritual community around and within the space of the Zen poem where a ritual of deep reflection and introspection is performed on the printed page. Seen in this context, neither "Zen" nor "poem," is a singular, fixed "entity," McNiece further posits his claim in his Introduction to *America Zen: A Gathering of Poets*, confirming that art, like spiritual practice, for di Prima, attains greater presence and vivacity through human connectivity and shared lived experience. Neither Buddhism nor poetry is a fixed essence, di Prima's longtime teacher Suzuki Roshi agreed, though an essence of energetic livelihood, we might contend, does lie in the wake of what a poet hints at or says as he or she meditatively writes. For di Prima, then, both spirituality and art are spaces where she can explore the ink-stained essences of a "self" in "process," to borrow a phrase from the Buddhist, African-American author, Charles Johnson. Citing Johnson, in her essay titled, "What does Buddhist practice mean to North American Women?" Susanne Mrozik affirms that, for Buddhists, "self is not product, but process, not a noun, but a verb" (5). This sentiment pointedly describes di Prima's view of the self, both in "Visit to Katagiri Roshi," and in her poetry at large because di Prima, through her senses, continually explores the ever-evolving definition of "self" in a dynamic, mutable, and transient world. The self, for di Prima, is continually growing in "morsels" of time, interminably taking shape, coming into, and out of, view. The self is the site to which the poet/practitioner continues to return, and continues to "visit" the malleable site of self in spite of potentially paralyzing disappointments, hoping always to make a new discovery of sight, taste, speech, or sound.

Furthermore, like McNiece, himself a poet and Zen practitioner, di Prima manifests herself here in "Visit to Katagiri" as a believer in the notion that a poem is indeed a space where voices, spirits, and presences can "merge" and share the space of the page, a poetic space for di Prima that is co-occupied by linguistic consciousness and spiritual belief. "A poem is both the practice of words and the wave of vibration opening wormhole into consciousness," McNiece poetically observes, and di Prima's dialogue-with-Zen-teacher-in-verse here is indeed both an informal, linguistically un-premeditated, hand-penned journal-entry written on the road, and a sensitive and revelatory narrative of a singular and savory moment of *satori*, or consciousness-opening, for a woman struggling with her own daily, devotional practice (19). Moreover, what makes the lines of this Zen poem "vibrate" for us under the cadence of their own quiet music, is the way di Prima's private concerns about spiritual devotion are infused with her more public or global concern for "the hungry people" in starving nations who have little in the way of nourishment or sustenance (reflecting di Prima's hunger for an end to poverty and human suffering). It is for this reason, ostensibly, that Katagiri Roshi suggests sitting "ten minutes, five minutes," to di Prima, meditating in smaller "morsels," allowing each increment of deep sitting to serve as a vehicle for ultimate mindfulness and prayer for those who are starved. Di Prima's concern for the "hungry," emblematic of the Buddha's own concern for the meek and the impoverished, is one that pervades her poetry at large, and it is with unrelenting criticism of her own country, the United States, that di Prima questions "America like a sponge / soaking up" the world's resources. Here, as in earlier poems (and interviews) the poet's use of the tactile and visual image of a "sponge / soaking up" the world's resources allows us to understand the extent to which di Prima fears capitalism's tendency to wring and re-soak its "sponge" again and again in the world's water reserve, its vat of resources.

Thus, while the poet's concern over the disproportion of her meditation, and her anxiety over the world's hunger crisis appear to be the sources of her growing dejection, as both her conversation with her teacher, and the poem itself, progress, the speaker realizes that she's "on the road"—both the literal road she's traveling through America as a touring poet and teacher, and also the tumultuous road of the inner life—to continue energetically "transferring" the "gifts" of creativity, compassion, and perception to others. In lines that resonate with deep spirituality, the speaker has a realization:

> As I talk, it becomes OK...
> ...I even understand....
> why I'm on the road.
> As we talk a community, a
>   transfer of energy
> takes place.
> It is *darshan*, a blessing,
> transmission of some basic joy
> some ways of seeing.
> LIKE A TANGIBLE GIFT IN THE HAND
>   in the heart.
> It stays with me. (22, 24, 26-35)

These final stanzas of "Visit" are exemplary of Diane di Prima's openness as a poet, an illumined self intimately connected to the world it inhabits as well as the spiritual and poetic voices that inhabit it. The very "TANGIBLE GIFT" that the speaker holds in her "HAND" and creates "by hand" (as she says in her Naropa lecture) and within her heart at poem's end, is one that "stays with her," and remains tangible precisely because its value is inestimable. The gift that di Prima has received, both from her teacher, and from her engagement with writing, is the enduring sacredness of her own human imperfection, her sudden recognition that perfection is beyond tenability, and that is "OK." The gift in her hand is therefore the gift of understanding, a kind of elastic compassion that an imperfect but compassionate Buddhism and a self-abnegating, self-seeking poetics make possible for speaker, reader, Zen teacher, poetic community, and Zen sangha. Additionally, the gift in her hand is not her hand's capacity for clinging and attaching selfishly to people, places, or things it has come to depend upon. The gift in the hand is instead the gift that the hand keeps giving away, keeps passing on, keeps letting go. It remains "in the heart," and "stays" with the speaker, precisely because it must be relinquished and shared with others. Poetry, for instance, remains somewhat discreet, until it is published and then offered away to the world (as seventeenth century poet, Anne Bradstreet similarly intimated in her poem, "The Author to Her Book"). Meditation is largely solitary and has the practitioner in the keep of its trance or hold, until the "silver bell" of the monastery rings and awakens the meditator from the depths of his or her breathing. Energy itself is stored temporarily but is then eventually transferred through the inevitable process of motion. Therefore, what we learn, by poem's end, is that all is temporary; life is in fact shifting, transitional in nature. Things are given, and things are taken, and a wise woman lets this process run its course without resisting the fluid physics of being. It can therefore be said that the realization di Prima comes to, at the end of "Visit to Katagiri Roshi," is perhaps the most important of her Zen recognitions, visible or audible, throughout her Buddhist poetry. Here, hands and eyes are agents in the speaker's achievement of satori, a sudden flash of insight that brings on a deep awareness of selfhood rooted in utter selflessness. Selfhood is the gift one receives when one has given oneself completely away by mustering up the courage to transcend fears, anxieties, preoccupations, and delusions that inhibit total immersion in the world.

Finally, the speaker of the poem experiences a deep transfer of energy between student and teacher akin to the Hindu experience of "darshan" which, for people in India, "refers especially to religious seeing" and the "visual perception of the sacred" (Eck 4). In India, sacred sight is gained when devotees exchange gazes with the images of deities in hope of receiving the "blessings of the divine" (4). So, when di Prima speaks here, in a kind of diction that reflects a hybrid religiosity, a pluralism of Eastern spiritual imagery melding Zen and Hindu thought, she seeks to evoke the idea that the intimate exchange she has had with Katagiri is akin to the exchange of visual energy that a devotee experiences before the image of the divine in India. Katagiri, like Suzuki, is thus given a divine presence in di Prima's poetry; however, the divinity she ascribes to these Zen Masters, these spiritual teachers, is hardly hierarchal. To the contrary, these Zen teachers stand (or sit) at eye level with the poet, making the transfer of spiritual energy and human compassion equal, reciprocal. Her relationship to both Suzuki and Katagiri is reflexive, refractive, circular, and continuous. They see into each other's lives, and collectively imbue life around them with energy, meaning, and deep purpose, as evidenced by the tangible gift the Zen poem has left in the reader's hand.

Conclusion: "Raindrops Melting in a Pond": Zen Energy Absorbed and Transferred

Reading with wide eyes, attuned ears, and receptive hands, we come to see, in turn, that Diane di Prima's Beat Zen poetry is indeed a poetry that derives spiritual meaning from a deep level of sensory awareness and physical perceptivity. Time and again in di Prima's markedly Zen-engaged poems, and in her Zen-related interviews, the poet stresses the profound role that image-making plays in the construction of personal and communal meaning. More specifically, for di Prima, a westerner practicing Zen Buddhism in America, sensory image-making becomes a means through which to access a mode of spirituality outside the sphere of her New York upbringing. Imagery becomes the poet's way of drawing lines and carving out space for herself within the spiritually-informed aesthetic conversation that other Beat Buddhist poets Jack Kerouac, Allen Ginsberg, Gary Snyder, Philip Whalen, Gregory Corso, Lawrence Ferlinghetti, Lew Welsh, Lenore Kandel, Joanne Kyger, and later, Anne Waldman, were having throughout the fifties and sixties (and for some, into the seventies, and beyond). Whereas for Snyder, for instance, deep ecological concern might be a vessel through which to engage Zen, for di Prima it is artistic craftsmanship itself which remains the principal medium for addressing her Zen beliefs. Or whereas for Ginsberg, political affinities with Asia in the wake of WWII may be a chief means through which to embrace what Zen has to offer American poetry and the arts, it is, again, for di Prima, a deep devotion to a poetry made "by hand" in humble service and with marked gratitude toward her fellow poets, Zen teachers, and to the universe at large, which characterizes the spirit of her meditative, Zen poetry.

I do not wish here to create the impression that Diane di Prima has *only* produced a body of literature which is always quiet and meditative or spiritually, politically, or artistically understated. Indeed, some of di Prima's finest poems can be found in her politically engaged, verbally dynamic, rant-infused *Revolutionary Letters*, and some of her more experimental spiritual poems reflecting her turn to Tibetan Buddhism in the 1980s are some of di Prima's most glimmering, most evocative works to date. It could certainly be argued that di Prima does engage international conflict, environmental degradation, and the quest to further women's rights as profoundly as many of the poets noted in the previous paragraph. However, it is, in my estimation, what we might call the quieter, but imagistically potent and audiovisually precise di Prima who has been critically underappreciated. Additionally, while many of the poems I've cited here in this chapter appear in more recent anthologies of Buddhist poetry such as *Big Sky Mind: Buddhism and the Beat Generation* (1995), Anne Waldman's Buddhist-inflected *The Beat Book: Writings from the Beat Generation* (1996), *America Zen: A Gathering of Poets* (2004), *The Wisdom Anthology of North American Buddhist Poetry* (2005), there has yet to be serious critical work that historically, critically, or theoretically engages her oft anthologized Zen lyric poetry. Tony Trigilio, a well-known Beat-Buddhist literary critic, has produced an unpublished conference paper titled "Who did we pray to? Diane di Prima's *Loba*" presented at the 2008 Beat Symposium at Columbia College, Chicago, that provocatively addresses intersections between Buddhism and the feminine in di Prima's contemporary mythological epic poem, *Loba*. But Trigilio represents a very small group of critics who seem to be paying more attention to di Prima's employment of hybrid spiritualities and hybrid mythologies in *Loba*, and there is no visible scholarship placing her contemporary epic in conversation with her earlier Zen-engaged poems. Contrary to Ginsberg scholarship, for instance, few have tried to create a continuous narrative for di Prima's spiritual poetry to this point, which may be a clear indicator of the fact that scholarship on women of the Beat Generation is just now beginning its advance beyond its nascent stages (the field itself, little more than a decade old). Additionally, Anthony Libby's essay, "Diane di Prima: Nothing Is Lost; It Shines in our Eyes," touches on Buddhism as one aspect of di Prima's broad poetic repertoire, but only briefly discusses di Prima's Buddhist engagement in a single poem, "The Bus Ride."

Part of the impetus for this chapter, then, is to devote much more concentrated attention, to be much more mindful of, Diane di Prima's distinctly *Zen* poetry, which in my mind stands with integrity as its own poetic sub-genre in the corpus of her writing at large. Di Prima's Zen poetry glimmers with distinct sensitivity and verbal acuteness from out of the center of her catalogue of ambitious artistic output—an output that includes Tibetan poetry, Mythological poetry, political poetry, environmentally conscious poetry, confessional poetry, blues/jazz poetry, and literary-historical verse. Furthermore, performing a close and historically contextualized reading of what we might then call di Prima's "Zen-image" poems allows us to understand far more deeply, from a textual perspective, the way that Zen Buddhism really did influence American poetry after WWII. Di Prima's Zen-poetic encounter is more widely representative of a large group of American poets who lived on or traveled to the West Coast to encounter a level of spirituality which they felt was either personally or nationally absent in the years following the dropping of the atomic bomb on Hiroshima. In a certain sense, we might even read di Prima's Zen poems, poems like "For Suzuki Roshi," "I Fail as Dharma Teacher," "Tassajara, Early 1970s," "Visit to Katagiri Roshi," and some others, too, as di Prima's effort to generate a poetics of peace-making and reverence for life. Taken a step further, if Ginsberg's "Howl," for instance, is a kind of retaliatory, linguistic dynamite projected radically in the direction of those who decided to drop the atomic bomb in Hiroshima, might we begin to look at di Prima's Zen involvement—both her years reading, studying, and visiting D.T. Suzuki, Shunryu Suzuki, and Katagiri Roshi—as her own quiet, but ecstatically peaceful and harmonious attempt to "reach out her hand," to a fractured Japan decimated at the human-spirit level as a result atomic warfare? Even in her songs to "Baby—O," of the late fifties, where di Prima's Zen-poetic sensibilities are just beginning to take shape, we might see her treatment of the deceased child as an emblem of humanity at large after WWII, suffering interminably across a "gutted / breaking / globe." "Di Prima Zen," like "Suzuki Zen," is therefore a Zen of compassion, a globally conscious Zen that crosses cultural boundaries, East and West.

In a sense, what is most remarkable about Diane di Prima's Zen poetry influenced by her years as a meditator throughout the 1960s is, paradoxically, its ability to voice itself powerfully without drawing attention to itself, without dwelling egoistically on the fact of its very lyric potency. Unlike some of her Beat contemporaries, whose voices were perhaps louder and projected more forcefully than her own, di Prima's work has an auditory spiritual power that rises up out of moments of deep internal silence, as we see, for instance, when di Prima's speaker in "Tassajara" remembers the "echoes of voices already gone" that "hung on air." There is a way, indeed, in which life itself continues to "hang on air" in Diane di Prima's poetry, emboldening the very core of what Zen Buddhism holds as its principle belief: the power of the eternal present, a present that lives on precisely because meditation, creativity, and self-examination allow it to persist. Presence, the continuous moment, for Zen

Buddhists, does not continue to exist because we derive comfort in throwing half-earned faith to the great beyond hoping that memory's ecology might miraculously sustain itself. The power of living in the moment, to make memory part of each moment, arises from energy "latently" but vigorously "lying" deep within each of us, to evoke D.T Suzuki. This powerful dynamism of will moving centrifugally out of the nucleus of the inner life can be seen in di Prima's poem "For Suzuki Roshi," where the speaker's teacher returns to her to eat "Soba" in warm "broth" one last time. This moment occurs in the poet's life precisely because her repeated meditations and her continual belief in the endlessly "tangible gift" of human life have made it possible for her to receive life's continual energy, its gift of quiet force. As di Prima herself says, in her Naropa lecture, "By Any Means Necessary," "Energy of intent goes into the writing of the stuff" (207). What di Prima means here, is that if our intent is deep enough, focused enough, and generous enough, the poetry we write will absorb that intent as energy transferred from the senses, to the heart, to the spirit, to the brain, and back to the hand and out onto the page that waits to receive language's gifts. Seen in this way, the act of writing becomes synonymous with the act of living, the act of believing deeply in the universe's anatomical, intellectual and spiritual processes. The energy of di Prima's intent is made palpable in a poem like "For Suzuki Roshi," where the memory of the teacher is called up again, from just beneath the surface of a present tense he is continually swirling and continually simmering, traveling with her, in mind and spirit, along dharma road.

It is ultimately the dharma then, teeming with Buddha's golden light, that di Prima seeks to transmit to readers through her poetry, and it is the transmission of something very sacred and very alive that we receive when we read her poetry. Perhaps no image, no moment in her poetry quite so lucidly crystalizes or epitomizes what it is that di Prima's Zen poetry engenders within those of us who have stumbled onto its dharmic paths as the one we witness in the second stanza of "Three Dharma Poems." Provocatively, in the second of three haikus the poem features as a series, the poet, with complete command of the form, writes:

> Raindrops melt in the pond
> & it's hard to say
> just what "lineage" is. (4-6)

Here, in this American adaptation of the Japanese Haiku, (we might recall some of Kerouac's or Richard Wright's mid-century adaptations of a similar sort) di Prima melds image with philosophic statement to create a poem that directly speaks to Zen Buddhism's deepest concern: the question of "lineage" and the dharma's continual direct transmission from Buddha all the way to the present. However, the way in which the poet, an American Buddhist poet, speaks to the concern, is a complex one, an ambivalent one. On one hand, the poem's speaker may be critical of the way in which, following the death of teachers like Suzuki Roshi, Katagiri Roshi, or even Trungpa Rimpoche, Buddhism's transmission may in fact be "watering down," like previously singular and whole "raindrops," "melting" in a wider, American, spiritually-pluralistic "pond." Seen in this way, the poem takes on a wistful, if not pseudo-cynical tone about the future of Zen in America, about the future of Japanese-infused Zen poetry in American poetic circles.

On the other hand, though, the poem may be seen less as a critique of a changing poetic guard, less as a lament for the death of the Asian teachers who came to America and compassionately and ecstatically transmitted the dharma to American poets of the fifties and sixties. Seen in another light, these "raindrops," which we can hear clinking like little "silver bells" as they touch the pond surface and then diffuse, come to signify complete immersion, total environmental assimilation, as "water" inevitably "comes together with other water" (to borrow a line from Raymond Carver). This total merging of one body of water with another thus signifies, from this second perspective, the celebrated joining of one "lineage" with another. Consequently, it's "hard to say / just what lineage is" in America because "lineages," be they religious, cultural, or aesthetic, in this poet's native country, become entwined in time. Zen lineage, sewn like a luminous spiritual thread through the variegated tapestry of American poetry, significantly alters the tapestry's fabric and changes its design, just as American poetry, in turn, subtly reshapes and resews Zen's future "lineage" as it deepens and widens in the west. This synchronous movement, this ambivalent, hybrid exchange of spiritual and cultural values is emblematic of the levels of spiritual and aesthetic absorption we find in di Prima's highly imagistic Zen poetry. But the ambivalence evoked in this final poem is less indicative of di Prima's uncertainty about the future of American Zen poetry than it is her insistence on a capacious Buddhist "middle way" that makes room for multiple ways of seeing, hearing, and understanding the world as it shifts and changes its spontaneous trajectory, inexorably, through luminous, sonorous time.

PART TWO

Unlocking the Golden Gates

Lenore Kandel's Big Beat Buddhism and the Opening of Emerald Consciousness

Introduction: Lenore Kandel's Eastern Kingdom in the Zen West—Entering the Gates of Creation

In the opening paragraph of "INVITATION TO THE JOURNEY," her Preface to *The Collected Poems of Lenore Kandel*, Diane di Prima conjures a lucid and moving portrait of her relationship with Lenore Kandel in the late 1960s and provides a window to the world that she and Kandel co-inhabited in Zen San Francisco. With "homage" to her Beat sister and fellow Buddhist poet, di Prima recalls the following:

> When I first came from the East Coast to San Francisco on a reading tour in the Spring of 1968, the woman I stayed with ruled a magic kingdom, pristine as the heart of a jewel. She would have said emerald. I, perhaps, sapphire. Or ruby, for I dwell in fire. She in the heart of Venus/Isis; she dwelt in earth and in the middle of the air. I sought shelter from her, and she gave me shelter. I looked to the burning sidewalks of my broken stone island, she gave me welcome. Gave me a glass key to one of the gates of this four-walled city/temple. (xiii)

This passage has a way of transporting us back to Northern California, 1968. Better yet, the retrospective paragraph, sounding out of the past now like a piece of sensory prose poetry, has a way of bringing the past to *us*, a way of making di Prima's experience with Kandel one that is still living here in the Zen present of our twenty-first century lives. Rendering herself here as poet-vagabond, lighting out for a territory and rucksacking her way toward the mythic west, di Prima captures the late-Beat, pre-hippie ethos of the time in high relief. However, her description of the woman who awaited her in the west far exceeds the image of a tattered, nomadic, flower child or artist-vagabond. Quite contrarily, an enchanted poet-traveler full of wanderlust, di Prima depicts Lenore Kandel as the queen of a "pristine," "magic kingdom," a mythic goddess from another epoch, half "Venus," half "Isis," with a dark luminosity of one who held the "key" to a gleaming, golden-gated city facing the Pacific. Her recollection of her fellow Beat poet is framed by her experience in eclectic, mystic, psychedelic San Francisco, and within this frame of di Prima's memory, stands Lenore Kandel, holding a shimmering key to a world of deep wisdom, sacred knowledge, and potential enlightenment.

Additionally, di Prima's astute, imagistic, and elemental description of herself and Beat Buddhist gatekeeper, Kandel, allows us to make subtle but important distinctions between the personalities and poetic temperaments that each possessed as poets of the luminous late sixties. Indeed, di Prima is correct in her assessment that Kandel's mythopoetic, spiritual kingdom was a "pristine" one at the heart of an "emerald" literary movement, glistening with religious receptivity, a precious "jewel" of new artistic allure shimmering with all the possibilities that mythology, Buddhism, and Olsonian ideas about poetry as an open field had to offer these westward poets. Di Prima's own poetic and spiritual world, as she remembers it, was more like one encased in "sapphire," "burning all the way through" (as Suzuki Roshi implored) with "ruby" red intensity and eagerness to learn about what Suzuki's Zen Buddhism brought from Japan could provide for her, both artistically and personally. For if di Prima learned from Shunryu Suzuki Roshi that Zen meditation and Zen mindfulness allow an individual to "burn all the way past the barrier of the ego and through false preconceptions of the self", then Kandel, whom Brenda Knight tells us also studied with Suzuki in San Francisco, learned that within the "pristine" but earthy heart of Zen Buddhism lay arteries in which there seemed to flow a deeper knowing, channels of being coursing with ecstatic awareness and further spiritual possibility (280). Moreover, within the "shelter" of Kandel's "kingdom" of transformative, "dynamic," blue-and-yellow-mineral-infused, emerald-green, di Prima found herself opening with Kandel's "glass key" what Aldous Huxley called the "doors" of imaginative "perception." However, whereas di Prima's own poetry of the 1960s, we have seen, is primarily a Zen aesthetic "broth," simmering above the "ruby" fire of her own Pound-inflected poetic imagination, Lenore Kandel's majestic, but eccentric kingdom of exploratory Buddhist poetics can be said to resemble more a Whitmanesque spiritual elixir in which this "word alchemist," Kandel, was stirring and then "spinning meaning" in what Ronna C. Johnson has called a "dynamic" aesthetic "kinesis" (100).

In this chapter, I want to adopt Johnson's notion that, in her poetry, Kandel is "spinning" poetic "meaning" in a spiritual, sexual, and politically-charged, "dynamic kinesis"; however, whereas Johnson utilizes this dynamic phrase to address the way Kandel spins an authentic web of "Psychedelic Poetics," Tantric, "Cosmic Erotica," and controversial "Sexual Politics" in her historically significant 1966 collection of poems titled *The Love Book*, I want to appropriate and expand the register of Johnson's phrase to illuminate the ways Kandel spins and then stirs what I would call her "elixir" of "dynamic," "hybrid eastern religiosity" and "porous, shifting Buddhisms" in her poetry, and in particular, in her 1967 collection, *Word Alchemy*. Although a few years have passed since the long-awaited release of Kandel's *Collected Poems* (2012), and a little over a decade since Kandel's own passing after years of health complications resulting from a motorcycle accident she endured in 1970, there exists still far too little work on Kandel, and, in particular, on the poems in *Word Alchemy*, one of the more aesthetically groundbreaking and underappreciated volumes of American Buddhist poetry after WWII. Consequently, my impetus for writing this chapter is threefold. First, I wish to use the space of this chapter to expand the very limited critical reception and contextual understanding of Kandel's work and build upon the work of Brenda Knight, Marc Olmsted, and Ronna Johnson in order to give greater voice to Kandel's Buddhist poetry, both in *Word Alchemy*—a volume of poetry that reveals a more mature and nuanced poet richly immersed in multiple Buddhist idioms at once—and in her work at large. Second, I want to shed light on the way in which Kandel's poetry, like di Prima's, is rooted in the Zen Buddhism of Shunryu Suzuki and the San Francisco sixties, (and D.T. Suzuki's Zen Buddhism of the fifties) while also highlighting the way that Kandel's poetry crosses the Beat Zen nexus and travels across the thresholds of Tantric (Vajra) and Tibetan Buddhism by drawing on symbols and artistic images central to these branches of Buddhist faith as they manifest in Kandel's poems. Finally, I want to demonstrate the ways Kandel is at once a definitive Beat Buddhist poet, but also a unique and spiritually complex *American* poet in her own right, a woman with a deep belief in the notion that a poet never should compromise his or her own vision, even in a world that threatens a poet with spiritual or verbal censorship.

Lenore Kandel's uncompromisingly experimental, incantatory, harrowing, tender, and reverential poetry is, therefore, what di Prima herself says it is in her Preface of "Homage to Lenore Kandel." Kandel's poetry is, as di Prima posits, made of both "earth" and "air," or sky. The earth, in Kandel's work, represents the Buddhist belief in the simple majesty of earthly, human life teeming with energy in the moment here and now (which is epitomized by the Buddha himself, who pointed to earth as his witness in the moment of enlightenment). On the other hand, the sky, for Kandel, signifies the Buddhist notion that there exist numerous realms of consciousness in the universe that we humans might access if the "air" of the mind remains clear and open enough to life's vast horizon of spontaneous, creative possibilities. This vast, clear horizon, for Kandel, resembles her teacher's, Shunryu Suzuki Roshi's, notion of "big mind," or "big sky mind," which he explains in detail in a lecture titled "Control," in *Zen Mind, Beginner's Mind*:

> The true purpose [of Zen] is to see things as they are, to observe things as they are, and to let everything go as it goes. This is to put everything under control in a wider sense. Zen practice is to open up your small mind. So concentrating is just an aid to help you realize "big mind," or the mind that is everything... We should acquire this kind of perfect freedom. (16-17)

The "perfect freedom" of Kandel's "big mind" allows her to keep all options open as a poet, and these options are open to her precisely because she is in touch with what Suzuki would call the basic "rules" of meditation and mindful living, what Kandel might herself have called the basic "rules" of a mindful poetic craft. Kandel's artistic craft thus not only embodies what Marc Olmsted might call the "primordially ground[ed]" and concrete aesthetic praxis embraced by Beat poets like Diane di Prima, Gary Snyder, Joanne Kyger, or Lew Welch, but also embraces Shunryu Suzuki's notion of a vast, "big mind" flowing with uninterrupted clarity and creative freedom. Lenore Kandel's poetry navigates between these two realms of ground and air or sky, fluidly oscillating between poetic craft grounded deep in the humility of mineral earth and an uncompromisingly wide spiritual vision vast as what Kandel sees as an "etheric," infinity of sky.

A Luminous "Sun" on the "Bridge of Capricorn": Lenore Kandel's "Etheric," "Infinite" and "Unabashed" Buddhist Spirituality

If we are to handle with aesthetic sensitivity and deepened historical awareness the poetry that Kandel came to write in her unpublished Buddhist poetry and her 1967 spiritually "dynamic" collection *Word Alchemy*, it is worth saying some things about a few of the significant personal and poetic events that preceded the publication of Kandel's important work in the area of American Buddhist poetics. In her introductory note to Kandel's poems in her 1996 anthology *The Beat Book*, poet and editor Anne Waldman affirms that Lenore Kandel was indeed a "legendary presence in San Francisco in the fifties and sixties," a description matching the "legendary," "majestic" aura with which di Prima surrounds Kandel in her Preface recounting her arrival in San Francisco in the spring of 1968 (273). In fact, Waldman expands upon her short introduction to a poet who, in her own words, became "a recluse" after 1970, when she recalls a small autobiographical window Kandel provided in 1967. In poetic fashion, Kandel explains:

> I was born under the sign of Capricorn originally in New York City and later in Pennsylvania, Los Angeles, San Francisco and other locations. I am no longer a professional belly dancer, school bus driver, or choir singer. I stand witness to the divine animal and the possibility of the ecstatic access of enlightenment. (qtd. in Waldman 273)

In this concise autobiographical excerpt (for Kandel, these are few and far between) we are offered a fleeting glimpse into the kind of life that Lenore Kandel lived in the years leading right up to the publication of *Word Alchemy* (1967), the sort of life which is virtually always on the move. We can see from the brief excerpt, Kandel liked living in various places, just as she found enjoyment dwelling in various forms of Buddhism, be they Tantric, Zen, or Tibetan. Here, an eclectic mélange, a hybrid collage, of living, traveling, working, and worshiping comes to the forefront for the reader. The eccentric mix of vocations Kandel performed throughout her life, alongside her principal vocation as poet, tells us not only that she would do what she had to in order to make ends meet (a necessity for a full-time poet), but also that Kandel's interests were far-reaching and not discriminative. Born under the sign of Capricorn, a sign often associated with persistence and industriousness, Kandel proves here not to be above any line of menial, physical, or spiritual work. Instead, she reveals herself as a person who did what she had to do, mirroring in many ways the kind of staunch belief that Diane di Prima has expressed in the power of artistic handcraft, in poetry as a continuous and humble form of energized manual labor. Additionally, astrology itself was almost a vocation for Lenore Kandel, as evidenced by the way it informed the striking, final poem in her *Collected Poems*, titled "Winter Solstice, 1975," where the poet, at the end of the Vietnam War, sings to make sense of a life of perplexing "extremes":

> The sun stands on the bridge of Capricorn
> Saturn's unyielding fulcrum
> a tightrope stretched between practical trivia
> and the etheric infinity of unlashed spirit...
>
> This is a season of extremes
> Sudden gains and sudden losses
> Insights and intuitions both blessing and denying.
> (1-4, 16-18)

Even in this previously unpublished poem that succeeded both *The Love Book* and *Word Alchemy* we can hear evidence of Kandel contemplating, at season's turn, the undulating and ceaselessly shifting nature of life. Like the individual singer's voice that rises and then falls in sync with a choir, and like the belly of the fluid dancer shifting perpetually from side to side, Kandel's life and poetic vision embody a "dynamic kinesis," a perpetual state of motion. The small but significantly related vocations which Kandel practiced figure as gems of contextual significance that illuminate the kind of American Buddhist poet she was—a poet interested in the "kinesis" of both language and nature as well as the dynamic force of the body moving in time and through space.

While it certainly provides "access" into the eclectic, off-"Beat" life Kandel lived between two coasts, the above passage more specifically speaks to the ways in which Lenore Kandel fully embodied the holy vision of the American Buddhist poet. For one thing, as alluded to in the previous paragraph, the autobiographical excerpt presents a poet with a definitively Zen temperament—spontaneous, grounded, humble, mindful, and cognizant of the simple fact that "enlightenment" is accessible right here in daily life, and can be found even in the midst of our rudimentary "animal" (which is to say, "human") activities. After all, it was enlightenment which Kandel herself was seeking through the medium of poetry, as we will see later in her oft-anthologized "Enlightenment Poem." Poetry was to Kandel (and di Prima) what Zen practice was to her teacher Suzuki Roshi: a means by which to shatter the illusion that we humans are anything more than what we are in our earthly forms, and that this being human is a form of divinity itself. Yet the passage from Kandel is also quintessentially Buddhist in a markedly subtler way. Nowhere in the diction Kandel uses does she say that she "moved" or "traveled" from city to city, or state to state. Conversely, Kandel says that she was born "under" the "sign of Capricorn" (which is to say "in service" to the sign, or to the very cosmos itself), "in

New York City, Pennsylvania, Los Angeles, San Francisco, and other locations." The uninterrupted syntactical continuity of the proper nouns she uses, the various locales she lists in the sentence, gives off the verbal impression that Kandel was in fact "born" again, perhaps "re-incarnated," in all of these places, each time she relocated. Said another way, these various "locations" in which Kandel lived merge to form one continuous constellation of living and being, intimately and irrevocably connected in one spontaneously linked, luminous, geographic destiny. The trajectory of Kandel's movement along this constellation, and across a land of stars and stripes itself mirrors the spiritual trajectory that her poetry follows in the 1960s as she moves from the East Coast to the West Coast of the U.S., which is to say, paradoxically, further from a Western European ethos and closer to Asia's Far-Eastern sensibilities.

"The Temple and the God Entire": Kandel's Early Tantric/Zen Vision and the Awakening of a Spontaneous Subjectivity

Crossing geographic, spiritual, and social boundaries is one of the hallmarks of Lenore Kandel's personal and poetic life, and her willingness to transcend barriers and merge seemingly incongruous concepts is evident in both *The Love Book* and in *Word Alchemy*. As Brenda Knight observes in *Women of the Beat Generation*, "Lenore Kandel's poetry seeks to bridge the chasm between the sacred and the sexual, between religion and the eroticism of the body replete with Tantric symbolism, her works reflect the Buddhist influence as well as the corporeal" (279). Knight's lucid and accurate description of Kandel's ability to "bridge" a "chasm" amid the "sacred and the sexual" in a country where the union of body and spirit is a virtual taboo can be seen almost immediately in *The Love Book's* opening poem, "God/Love Poem," where the poem's speaker tenderly and sensuously recalls that

> there was a time when gods were purer
> / I can recall nights among the honeysuckle
> Our juices sweeter than honey
> / we were the temple and the god entire /
>
> I am naked against you
> and put my mouth on you   slowly
> I have longing to kiss you
> and my tongue makes worship on you
> you are beautiful. (18-26)

Here, in the third and fourth stanzas of the volume's opening poem, lines of the utmost delicacy unfold like the petals of the lotus upon the page. In the middle of a poem that begins, initially, with the somewhat graphic, but still tender act of lovemaking between a man and a woman, Kandel's speaker's voice resonates with a sweetness and directness reminiscent of Keats or Elizabeth Barrett Browning, but the diction itself is wholly modern, wholly embracive of a minimalist, Zen honesty that pervaded American poetry of the 1960s and, to some degree, still does today. For Kandel's speaker, natural images of "honeysuckle" and "honey," half-rhyming across the lines, create a pastoral, almost Edenic scene in the reader's mind where the bodies of the lovers become flowers in a garden out of "time," a simpler time when the "gods" themselves were "purer," unblemished and undistorted by demagoguery or the mere fact of elapsed time. To Kandel, these ancient, unnamed "gods" of old are "purer," precisely because the separation between god and man or woman did not exist as noticeably as it does in the post-lapsarian, twentieth century her speaker inhabits—a century where some churches and "temples" have become houses of unconscious "worship" and diminished feeling, human faith ravaged by the imminent threat of atomic war. Conversely, in the Tantric-Indian/Christian-Edenic/Greek-Pagan hybrid realm Kandel imagines here in "God/Love Poem" (a realm in which the words "God" and "Love" are virtually synonymous, divided only by a thin slash), it is possible for a man and a woman to constitute "the temple" *and* "the god entire" without separation, or what Zen teacher Suzuki Roshi might have called a dualism falsely conceived.

In true *Zen* fashion, Kandel disrupts the conventionally codified schism between "god" and "temple," by suggesting that a total immersion of two lovers' bodies itself forms the surrounding "temple" that allows for a fluid, shifting, moving "god" to flow within the divine architecture of their converging and joining bodies—through the kinetic atmosphere of our collective, shared, human lives. It is precisely the nakedness of the speaker's body against her lover's which becomes, "Holy, Holy, Holy...," as Ginsberg chants in his own corporeally operatic and controversial poem, "Howl." With Ginsberg, Kandel is in full agreement that "The world is holy. The soul is holy/ The skin is holy" ("Footnote to Howl" 1-3). In Kandel's own love ode to the holy "soul" and "skin," her amorous speaker, pressed "against" the weight of her lover's body, comes to recognize her own subjectivity and the fuller potential of her own sacred human autonomy. Her willingness to transcend the boundaries of acceptable printed language, to "dive" as Adrienne Rich would say, "into the wreck" of Western-patriarchal, socio-linguistic construction, allows her to discover what is wholly/holy beyond language, which is the "mouth" itself moving "slowly" like the lovers on Keats' Grecian Urn, with ecstatic anticipation toward a long-awaited, ritual "kiss." Thus, when the speaker proclaims "my tongue makes worship to you / you are beautiful," the imagery is not a confirmation of the female speaker's subservience, but rather an affirmation (a vehement "yes") of the "tongue's" own divinity, its own ability to generate a second language beyond words, one that is both physical *and* ethereal, in service to both the poem's sacred, textual body and the lover's consecrated flesh. Her lover's body is "beautiful" precisely because it has been worshipped without a language laden with what Suzuki calls "preconceived notions" about beauty in his lecture "No Trace." This speaker is quite literally discovering (or at least re-discovering in her memory) what the lover's body means to her right before us on the "skin" of the page. This act is a Zen-performative one, one worthy of "worship" precisely because of the unpremeditated, Beat-spontaneity with which the poem's speaker engages a bi-"lingual" act of love making and verse-making dually constituted.

Though at first glance it could appear that Kandel's implementation of what Knight calls "Tantric symbols" or Tantric concepts in "God/Love Poem" is a distinct divergence from Zen Buddhism's less conceptual, more pragmatic nexus of spirituality, what is really at work in "God/Love Poem" is Kandel's willingness to embrace what Marc Olmsted, in "Genius All the Time: The Spontaneous Presence and Primordial Ground," would call the overlap or reciprocity between Zen Buddhism and Tantric Buddhism within the canon of Beat poetry. In his article, Olmsted begins by making the following important claim, one that has a great bearing on the way in which we read Kandel's work. Significantly, Olmsted asserts that

> The Beat literary movement cannot be understood in the fullest sense without some examination of Buddhism, particularly in the forms that were available to these mysthinauts. The poet Anne Waldman, commenting on what constitutes Beat, perceives "an as yet unacknowledged body of uniquely articulated and salutary dharma poetics — that derives from Buddhist psychology and philosophy."...[F]ollowing Waldman's thinking one can conclude that the Beat literary movement involved a sacred worldview linked with the aspiration to actualize compassionate and empathetic conduct, an intuitive Tantric Buddhism....While it is Zen Buddhism that is most frequently and legitimately associated with the Beat movement prior to the 1960s and 1970s, both Zen and Tantric Buddhism share many philosophic parallels. Simply stated, their highest views regard "enlightenment" as already completely and unshakably present (if obscured) to be realized rather

than polished into existence. (179)

Though in his article he focuses primarily on Ginsberg's (not Kandel's) hybrid, spontaneous "dharma poetics," Olmsted's ability to draw together the Zen and Tantric elements dynamically stirred within the elixir of Beat Buddhist poetry allows us to understand the porous relationship that Kandel justifiably perceived between the two schools of Buddhist thought—Zen and Tantric. In her attempt to utilize poetry to draw attention to the way in which "enlightenment" is indeed "already completely and unshakably present to be realized" in mind, body, and spirit, here on earth, Kandel not only creates what Waldman dubs a "uniquely articulated and salutary dharma poetics" that embody Buddha's own life and teachings, but also creates a jointly practical and ethereal, hybrid American Buddhist poetics of the sixties that rivals Ginsberg's pluralistic open-verse corpus comprised of spiritually-porous poems like "Howl" and "Kaddish." Additionally, like Ginsberg and di Prima, Kandel, in both her Zen-Tantric *Love Book* poems, and in her largely Zen, Tibetan, spiritually pluralistic *Word Alchemy* proves that a Buddhist poetic corpus need not exclude sensory ecstasy and physical pleasure. To purposely exclude sensory experience from life—in both di Prima's and Kandel's views—would mean denying two foundationally human modes of experiencing life itself: sensory exploration and physical immersion in the world.

It is indeed a profoundly imaginative, sensory immersion—what Ronna C. Johnson calls 1960s mystic "Bacchanalia"—that we witness in the closing stanzas of Kandel's spiritually experimental "God/Love Poem" (Johnson 99). Investing herself completely in the act of lovemaking, Kandel's speaker crosses the threshold of the erotic and enters a "golden" city of flesh and spirit divine. With an increasingly sensual diction, and a breathless rhythm now, she writes:

> your body moves to me
> flesh to flesh
> skin sliding over golden skin
> as mine to yours…
> sliding…sliding…
> your face above me
>   is the face of all the gods
>   and beautiful demons…
> love touches love
> the temple and the god
> are one. (27-30, 37-39, 41-43)

Not a word is wasted here within the open field of Kandel's Tantric/Zen Buddhist performance of the sacred act of lovemaking. As the poem moves toward its final image of complete union and total immersion, it is simultaneously propelled by a Zen aesthetic minimalism and a Tantric, corporeal sensuality which seems to want to burst forth from within the tense movement of these short, attenuated lines of poetic composition. More specifically, it is the poem's sensory, emotive ecstasy that wants to project sideways with a spontaneous euphoria resulting from the shared act of lovemaking; however, the austere, yet fluid and slender, cascade of form moving in an intermittent diagonal rush down the page seems to refuse each individual line's desire to spring, dart, and expand horizontally toward the page's right margin. This is a result of the fact that the speaker is invited, again and again (line after subsequent line), to return to the original call of the lover's body, "flesh" beckoned by "flesh," "body" returning intuitively and without premeditation to the temple of the lover's "golden skin," now glimmering with anticipated awakening at the start of each new line. "Sliding" down the speaker's body, it is the lover here who serves as agent to spiritual awakening, "joining" the speaker with awareness itself. Her awareness, like the look in the lover's "eyes," is the recognition that the "face" of unconditioned "love" is no two-headed monster, born out of society's binarily-constructed, dualistic view of love. Instead, the lover's visage is a face beyond simple codifications of good and evil; rather, it is the "face of all the gods / and beautiful demons," a deity with a thousand faces merging in ecstatic union as the speaker enters a realm of Zen purity and Tantric harmony devoid of divisive categorizations. In this realm of pleasure, solemnity, darkness, luminosity, and utter sublimity, "love touches love," folding back on itself like one body over another. This realm is what Olmsted would call a "primordial," atemporal ground, an immediacy that, for these lovers, is at once nowhere visible and yet also totally visible within the ellipses and various syntactical absences of the poem's Olson-inflected field. Thus, man and woman, speech and silence, form and formlessness, and "temple" and "god" not only merge through the poem's linguistic space of absence/presence, but finally *are* "one." This realization of oneness is at last paradoxically solidified when it is diffused and then communally shared by the speaker, lover, reader, poet, and world at the poem's end.

The "Electric" Shock of a Radically Harmonious Poetry: Lenore Kandel's Holy Yawp of 1966

We might say, then, that what is most controversial or unorthodox to the twenty-first century reader of Kandel's "God/Love Poem," is not, as Ronna Johnson reminds us, its "graphic" portrayal of "heterosexual love" couched in a language of "Beat poetics" and "Eastern mysticism" (90). Conversely, it is more so the author's radical Buddhist re-visioning of the American body within a Zen/Tantric, non-dualistic, multi-spiritual architecture that more significantly disturbs conservative ideas about what an American poem should look like or sound like. It is therefore not only the poem's language, but also its ostensibly threatening spiritual indeterminacy that has confounded critics for decades. While there may in fact be no clear link between *The Love Book's* overt challenge to the American religious establishment and its eventual seizure by police (and the ensuing trial that took place as a result of claims that the text was obscene), the poem's erotic religiosity certainly caused quite the stir in mid-sixties San Francisco. For as Ronna C. Johnson tells us in "Lenore Kandel's *The Love Book*: Psychedelic Poetics, Cosmic Erotica, and Sexual Politics in the Mid-Sixties Counterculture," Kandel's 1966 collection was "confiscated by San Francisco police for obscenity, repeating a decade later the seminal Beat event of the *Howl* seizure," which also resulted in a long, literary censorship trial (90). Expounding in greater specificity on the reasons for the text's seizure, Johnson goes on to say that,

> *The Love Book's* origins in female sexuality and sexual emancipation, its publicized seizure and obscenity trial, its female author's controversial use of profane sex words in poetry—these illuminate Kandel's Beatness and her role in the transformation of Beat Generation ethics into the rebel freedoms of the '60s counterculture..... In the '60s counterculture from which *The Love Book* issued, sex underwent Edenic reinvention and acquired a veneer of innocence, drug use focused on consciousness expansion through peyote or LSD, and Hindu cosmology and Tantric yoga practice augmented Buddhist devotion. (90, 98)

Johnson's contextual overview serves to "illuminate" the physically and spiritually experimental landscape in which Lenore Kandel found herself in mid to late 1960s San Francisco. Johnson's overview also serves to remind us that Kandel was indeed not the only poet partaking in the Beat Generation's project of "consciousness expansion," a project in which Diane di Prima herself was admittedly invested, as she makes clear in her Preface to *The Collected Poems of Lenore Kandel*. Yet there is also a way in which such a highly sociocultural perspective might cause one to miss the deeper spiritual and aesthetic implications of Kandel's involvement in a literary scene that did, in some ways, contradict its own vow to holy life by undeniably engaging in "drug usage." More specifically, Johnson's perspective, contextually lucid as it is, neglects to mention the way in which Lenore Kandel helped unlock the visionary gates of Buddhist American poetics for her fellow writers with the "glass key" of her own creative receptivity and her awareness of the sacred "golden skin" of language—in all of its divine beauty and its seemingly "demonic" incarnations.

Moreover, incorporating and embodying a hybrid, Zen/Tantric Buddhist aesthetic allowed Lenore Kandel to speak with both unmitigated honesty and unrelenting delicacy about the sanctity and holiness of the body in a century which paid witness to innumerable acts of bodily and spiritual degradation. Kandel's poetry, like Whitman's a century before, casts an elegant, celebratory, and disruptive yawp, similar to, but also distinct from Ginsberg's mantric "Howl," in the direction of Puritan America's unrelenting shame surrounding the body. For Kandel, who "became a Buddhist at the age of twelve," freeing the body, liberating it from shame, is as significant as freeing the mind from endless delusion (Knight 279). Like di Prima, Kandel was well aware of what D.T Suzuki meant when, in "The Sense of Zen," he proclaimed:

> This body of ours is something like an electric battery in which a mysterious power latently lies. When this power is not properly brought into operation, it either grows moldy and withers away or is warped and expresses itself abnormally. It is the object of Zen, therefore, to save us from going crazy or being crippled. This is what I mean by freedom giving free play to all of the creative and benevolent impulses inherently lying in our hearts. Generally, we are blind to the fact that we are in possession of all the necessary faculties that will make us happy and loving towards one another. All the

> struggles that we see around us come from ignorance.... When this cloud of ignorance disappears the infinity of the heavens is manifested, where we see for the first time into the nature of our own being. (3-4)

Kandel, like Whitman, and Suzuki, before her, is an American Buddhist poet-philosopher who "sings the body electric," one who recognizes the power lying dormant, but ready to flash awake within the frictional, atomic composition of the body's "charged battery." If the "object" of Zen, as Suzuki posits, is to "save us from going crazy," then recognizing the body's capacity for energetic, dynamic and "creative, free play" is the luminous road to sustained mental sanity and psychic healing. Recognizing the "necessity" of the body, Kandel thus renders the body once again for American readers and spiritual aspirants, as Suzuki recommends, as a source of unlimited happiness, benevolence, and love. The body, in Kandel's cosmic-corporeality, therefore becomes a vessel through which to transcend our seemingly interminable human struggles, the endless gyre of human ignorance, delusion, and bewilderment known to Buddhists as samsara. Additionally, it is interesting to note that when D.T. Suzuki speaks of Zen's ability to make "the cloud of ignorance disappear," he says that the cloud's dissolution allows "the infinity of the heavens" to be "manifested" before the devotee's (or the poet's) eyes. This description of the cloud's disappearance—ignorance's very dissipation—intimately connects to Kandel's own description of the sun's luminosity shining upon a world marred by incessant "practical trivia," innumerable human "losses," inconceivable political "extremes" and inevitable personal "denials" in the aforementioned "Winter Solstice" poem. More specifically, Kandel seems to suggest that in spite of these daunting human realities, life itself is also complementarily constituted by personal "gains," deep spiritual "insights" and creative, spontaneous "intuitions" that counterbalance suffering in an "etheric infinity of unabashed spirit." It is the very "infinity" of the human spirit, stretching out over the vast Buddhist "bridge" of human time and celestial/cosmic space that, for both Kandel and Suzuki, represents the luminescent potentiality of seeing "into the nature of our own being," into the very core of what Buddhists call our "Buddha Nature," "free" of "ignorance" that blinds us from "benevolent" self-awareness and awareness of others in the world around us. This is what Wordsworth, the Romantic seeker, termed "seeing into the life of things" in "Tintern Abbey."

It would appear then, after examining Kandel's "God/Love Poem," in addition to her autobiographical commentary and the language she uses in "Winter Solstice, 1975," that Marc Olmsted is indeed correct when he postulates that the "attraction of the philosophy and practice" of not only Zen Buddhism, but also Tantric Buddhism, "for many of the Beats, lies in Buddhism's exploration of the nature of awareness" (Olmsted 179). For Kandel, and for di Prima, becoming aware of the limits and potentialities of individual and collective human experience is the essential mineral "at the heart" of their "emerald" poetics. For Kandel in particular though, Tantric Buddhism proved particularly attractive, particularly liberating, in the way it posits "that the world of form is as sacred as the clear open space of the emptiness that is essence" (101). In other words, Tantric Buddhism provided a middle way for Kandel, a "bridge" between the "extreme" far shores of form—an indispensable necessity for any serious poet or artist—and formlessness—an irrevocable, elemental truth for any devoted spiritualist. Kandel's work in *The Love Book* can itself thus be seen as a vital literary bridge to her next collection of poetry, *Word Alchemy*, an even more spiritually variegated text sprayed with Vajra Buddhist, Zen Buddhist, Tibetan Buddhist, and even Hindu spiritual overtones. It is *The Love Book's* radical belief in the sacredness of lovemaking and the holy energy "lying latent" in the generative and expressive human body that paves the way for Kandel's even more nuanced, psychospiritually evocative verse that ensued.

Beyond Mountains Unaware: Kandel's "Dynamic," "Barrier-Breaking" Dakini

As we have seen thus far, the erotic, ecstatic, holy space of poetry, for Lenore Kandel, is a psychospiritual cosmos through which the poet can search the ethers of consciousness for unforeseen selves in the big sky of poetry's creative potential. The stanzas in Kandel's poems are, consequently, meditative constellations of transformative light where the poet emerges each time carrying new "essence[s]" of meaning as she burns comet-tailed toward a fiery awakening. While Kandel is, on one hand, the definitively autonomous, creative force of feminine, spiritual authority behind her poems, (refusing to "compromise" her hybrid spiritual vision) there is, on the other hand, a strong sense in her Buddhist-inflected verse, that language is shaping *her*, turning her life like a phrase in an unanticipated direction toward some new grammar of being. Said another way, Kandel's sense that new selves can take shape, that new modes of existence can spin into being "beyond" the mountainous barriers of conventional thought are perpetually on display in the Buddhist cosmos of her poetry. For as Kandel, herself, has written, in "Poetry in Never Compromise," the "direction" of a poet's "vision," "is beyond the limits of the conceivable. There are no barriers to poetry or prophecy; by their nature they are barrier breakers, bursts of perception, lines into infinity" (xviii-xix). This aesthetic statement from what we might consider Kandel's short, but provocative "manifesto" of poetry, encapsulates an essence of Kandel's poetic aims, a body of poetry replete with "bursts" and sprays of Buddhist insight and "perception," a poetry whose prophetic "lines" simultaneously circle back to touch Buddhism's "primordial ground" and extend forward into the infinite reaches of psychic space and yet-to-be-unveiled time. Time and again, moving as she does against the powerful, kinetic thrust of 1960s cultural orthodoxy and established ideas about what poetry should or should not be, Kandel reveals a willingness to transcend "barriers" or boundaries that stand in the way of her bold quest for personal and aesthetic liberation.

In the sections that ensue, I want to look first at one of Kandel's *unpublished* poems from the 1960s, titled "Songs of the Blue-Light Dakini," in order to foreground the way Kandel comes to challenge boundaries of consciousness and disintegrates barriers to spiritual creativity in *published* works such as "Enlightenment Poem," Small Prayer for Fallen Angels," and "Emerald Poem," (as well as some excerpts from Buddhist poems that appear in *Word Alchemy*, her second volume of poems). Though it's unfortunate that some of Kandel's finest poems, and, in my estimation, finest *Buddhist* poems, remained unpublished until after her death, we can utilize some of the conceptually, spiritually, historically, and philosophically revealing language in unpublished poems from Penny Press chapbook poems (as I illustrated earlier, with the poem "Winter Solstice, 1975") to help "bridge" important conceptual "gaps" in Kandel's work, and narrow the "chasm" created by spiritual complexities within Kandel's poetry and Beat poetry at large. Though it is impossible to rely on Kandel's unpublished poetry that spans at least forty-five years of reading, writing, and revising poems, Kandel's poems from little magazines and unpublished notebooks should be seen as small, but significant beams of light that help us shed greater contextual light on the aesthetic vision and poetic life of a writer who, as Anne Waldman has noted, lived as a recluse for the final thirty-plus years of her life. In a sense, poems like "Winter Solstice, 1975," "Song of the Blue Light Dakini," and "Holding" (which I will discuss at the end of this chapter) merge as a luminous constellation of Buddhist poems that help us more fluidly enter the gates of a collection like *Word Alchemy*, dauntingly hybrid in its rich elixir of Beat, eastern religiosities.

"Song of the Blue-Light Dakin," is representative of precisely the kind of thinking that pervaded 1960s San Francisco, a city whose gates were as wide and expansive as Shunryu Suzuki's seemingly limitless "big," Zen mind. "Blue-Light Dakini" is exactly the kind of poem that exemplifies the female Beat aesthetic of the sixties and seventies, the type of poem one might have encountered in San Francisco's *Oracle*, a risqué, Buddhist, artistic, and poetic underground newspaper that featured writers like Kandel, Ginsberg, Kerouac, and Snyder between the years of 1966 and 1967. Though we will look at one of these poems—Kandel's "Enlightenment Poem"—a bit later in this chapter, we can enter into Kandel's definitive, 1960s consciousness by hearing the voice of her "Blue-Light" speaker, who, in an ethereal, mystical tone of voice, seems to almost chant the following lines:

> beyond these mountains there are other mountains
> the substance is of a different texture
> some become star earth becomes cloud
> dust becomes prismatic flakes of light...
>
> beyond this body there are other bodies...
> flesh becomes space breath becomes time
> senses and perceptions become galaxies
> beyond these bodies there are others. (1-5, 8-10)

Hearing portions of the poem here allows us to visually and sonically process the ways the poem's repetitions are not only working to intensify its quiet but pronounced Zen Buddhist, minimalist form and its austere Zen tone, but also allow us to witness the poem's gradual accumulation of poetic vision and motion as the speaker's consciousness travels from the earthly, to the celestial, and the corporeal out into the far reaches of cosmic perception and cosmic time. Within the poem's atmosphere of dawn or dusk, "Blue-Light" imagining Kandel's speaker is a "Dakini," an ancient Indian female, Schneider tells us, who is "often found in the company of Gods" (82). But while Kandel's Dakini (perhaps Kandel herself, posing as Dakini), does appear to possess a link to an ancient world "beyond" isolating conceptual "mountains" and constricting notions about earthly "bodies," the word Dakini appears vested here with still more texture, more "body," than might appear to the reader's naked eye.

In Shambala's *Encyclopedia of Eastern Religions*, Schneider, an authority on Buddhist studies, informs us that in Tantric, or Vajrayana, Buddhism, which we now know Kandel studied and utilized in the writing of *The Love Book*, the Dakini is in fact "the inspiring power of consciousness, usually depicted in iconography as a semiwrathful female figure" (82). However, in Tibetan Buddhism, on the other hand, the Dakini, referred to specifically as *khadroma*, a term etymologically composed of *kha*—meaning "celestial space" or "emptiness," *dro*—signifying "walking" or "moving about," and *ma*—denoting "the feminine gender in the substantive form" (83). "Thus, the *khadroma*," Schneider explains, "is a female figure that moves on the highest level of reality; her nakedness symbolizes knowledge of truth unveiled" (83). Schneider's explication of the Dakini, or "khadroma," is useful in the ways it helps us identify the multifaceted religious lexicon, the various Buddhist idioms, from which Kandel drew her image of the "Blue-Light Dakini." To begin with, Schneider's definitions help us form a context for interpreting the thematic underpinnings of Kandel's Beat Buddhist poem. For example, if Kandel's Dakini is an agent or guide accompanying not a set of gods, but a sangha of questing *human* readers looking for a path out of delusion, then the poem's appeal to the sacred is vital to our own readerly attainment of enlightenment at poem's end. The Poet-Dakini is, in this view of the poem, precisely the one who can take us to the holy place beyond illusion, beyond spiritual conformity or confusion. The well-traveled, path-dwelling, ancient

Dakini is the one equipped to lead us beyond the "mountains" of inhibition, the walls that close off the peripheries of vision and erect what Kandel might have called "barriers" obstructing "awareness," sense, thought, and feeling, preventing humans from exploring the "texture" and "substance" of authentic consciousness. With the help of a Dakini, a female source of illumination holding out a map beyond the barriers of consciousness, the enlightenment-seeking reader/spiritual traveler is able to explore new constellations of identity, newly scattered essences, dust-blown and lit up like "prismatic flakes of light" in an existential/experiential/spiritual realm "beyond mountains."

From the standpoint of the poem's uniquely Buddhist, poetic diction, "prismatic," is precisely the right word here for a poem unfolding numerous hues of meaning and refracting various spiritual conceptual possibilities for its readers. For one thing, "prism" simultaneously evokes incandescent seeing and luminous awakening as the mind begins its travel across the barriers of perception and out into "other" realms of perceptivity. In another way, the word "prism" also serves to embolden Kandel's own multi-spiritual, "prismatic" poetics which draws from a number of Buddhist and Indian strands of thought. Seen more specifically in the "light" of Vajrayana/Tantric Buddhism, the prismatic poem might itself elucidate Kandel's desire to use poetry and art as a "hook knife"—the way the "semiwrathful" iconographical Indian Dakini sometimes does—as Schneider tells us, to slash the "demon of ignorance" and cut through nets of human obliviousness (83). Like the Dakini, Kandel (and her fellow Buddhist Beat poets) powerfully, but still calmly and collectedly, wields a pen like a fish hook that cuts through barriers of delusion and ignorance, what Trungpa Rimpoche (di Prima's and Ginsberg's late mentor) called "spiritual materialism." In contrast to a life lived solely within the "nets" or meshes of material reality—a life lived singularly in worship of the body and socially constructed notions of spiritual identity—Kandel's Dakini is an "inspiring power of consciousness," an agent in engaging in what Ginsberg in *The Beat Book* called the Beat Generation's "exploration of the [deeper] textures of consciousness" (noted in the previous chapter). Kandel's Dakini, like some of the chanting, ranting, bellowing poetic speakers of di Prima's Buddhist poems of the seventies and eighties, is calling us out of spiritual slumber here, beckoning us out of the low valley of mainstream culture's soporific doldrums, and out into the spaces where "earth becomes cloud," where one can escape samsara, allowing an authentic self to freely emerge without sociohistorical conditioning and preconceived ideas about the inner life.

Additionally, and perhaps more significantly, seen through the lens of Tibetan Buddhism, the poem's spiritual and conceptual resonances begin to deepen and widen with even greater elasticity. If the term Dakini, or "khadroma," holds within its linguistic construction, connotations of "emptiness" and energy "moving about"—matter moving kinetically across the dynamic cosmos and through the vastness of celestial space— then the poem and its starry syllables that float like meteors through its verbal atmosphere are also numerous Dakinis or agents of consciousness and catalysts of meaning-making and self-identification. In typical Beat-poetic fashion, as we see in the poems of di Prima, (and elsewhere in Ginsberg's poetry) language is a sacred tool with which one can unfold or peel back layers of consciousness; similarly, the Dakini—a sacred, religious personage—a luminous body of kinetic energy—is the one who unfolds or unveils the highest human "reality," the "naked" human "truth" that is an individual's fulfillment of his or her dharma. With the "veil" of Maya "drawn back" (to recall a phrase from the Japanese poet, Muso Soseki), the poem becomes the site where we can freely explore, with the help of the khadroma, a landscape of enlightenment beyond (but not ignorant of) the "flesh" where the "substance" or stuff of being human is of a wholly "different" conceptual "texture"—one diverse from the Zen/Tantric poetic body Kandel exposes in *The Love Book* (and diverse from di Prima's markedly Zen poetry of the sixties). In the realm to which the poem carries us, the new cosmic promontory to which the Dakini leads us, "mountainous," constrictive flesh is transformed and becomes porous open "space—" space for women to gain authorial autonomy, space for Beat poets to roam a cosmos of artistic possibilities. Within this more open field of space, "breath," the stuff of which "prana" (Buddhism's vital force of existence) is made becomes synchronous with "time"—not man-made-clock-time, but universal time, cosmic, non-linear temporality that flows on infinitely beyond our earthly provinces. It is in *that* range or field of cosmic time—a deeper, wider, vaster time—that our very "senses" and "perceptions"—all that we intuit and envision for our lives—become galaxies of creative potential and human vitality beyond the limitations of socially-constructed reason. "Beyond these bodies," beyond our own limited and flesh-encased, human bodies, but also beyond the "bodies" of newly discovered "galaxies," there are, at last, "others." There are other bodies of galaxies to explore, other planets, other stars, other lifeforms, other human bodies to "touch" (as Diane di Prima might say), "other" racial or sexual mountains to surpass, other bodies and forms of poetry to imagine and discover with new awareness beyond the confines of ignorance, suffering, artistic conservatism, and material illusion.

Crossing Psychic Thresholds: Blue-Light Awakening and the Attainment of Bodhi

If indeed attaining a state of "awareness," a realm of spiritual and artistic wakefulness where "stone becomes star" is the goal for Kandel's "Blue-Light" seeker, then certainly deep immersion in the world beyond her own ego is the means of achieving it. For as Kandel, in quintessential Zen fashion, writes in "Poetry Is Never Compromise"—her defense of poetic freedom of speech—"It feels so good that you can step outside of your private ego, and share the grace of the universe" (Waldman 275). While Kandel's own knowledge of the selfless, spiritual-quest-accompanying "Dakini"—in all of its varying Buddhist idioms—is definitely central to our understanding of the poem, there is yet another way in which we might spiritually place Kandel's "Song of the Blue-Light Dakini" within the context of larger Buddhist thought and practice. As mentioned earlier, it is safe to assume that Kandel, whose peers admired her for her vast knowledge of mythology and the world's religions, would have been well-acquainted with the "concise map of [the] journey to nirvana" the Buddha left behind in the "Vinaya Pitaka" (Easwaran 64). This verbal map, Eknath Easwaran tells us, chronicles the four stages of the Buddha's journey to enlightenment called the four *dhyanas*—a widely disseminated portion of the Buddha's teachings which derives from the Sanskrit word for "meditation" (64). "What the Buddha is giving us" in the dhyanas, Easwaran posits, "is something of universal application: a precise account of levels of awareness beneath the everyday waking state" (64). The dhyanas, like Kandel's poem written in stages of spiritual, psychic, and aesthetic consciousness-seeking, are a kind of map out of the self into complete wakefulness with the ultimate goal of total awakening "beyond mountains" of unawareness.

With this in mind, Kandel's "Song of the Blue-Light Dakini" takes on the form of a more "precise" engagement with Buddhist discourse. In a sense, Kandel, dressed here in the "prismatic," starry robe of the poet-guru, becomes for her reader what the Buddha is for his disciples and late followers, for those who continued to discover new states of "awareness" after his death. Like the Buddha's dhyanas, Kandel's Buddhist poems serve as what Easwaran would call a "field guide" for an exploration of the interiors of human consciousness. More specifically, Kandel's "Song" of the "Dakini," in which, let us not forget, the speaker is decisively feminine (a Dakini, and not a masculine Buddha), appears to deal specifically with the difficult journey one must make crossing from the second dhyana (the realization of non-duality, a realization of chief importance for Zen-Buddhists) into the third dhyana, the stage known as *bodhi*, "the illumination of consciousness that comes when the mind has been stilled" (255). This third stage of *bodhi* or "awakening" occurs only when one has attained "right attention" by "mastery" over "thought" and "senses" (the first dhyana) and when one has learned to swim "against the current," the concerted, deliberate effort to dissolve self-interest—the ego or "I" that prevents us from descending "steadily, step by step, into the depths of the unconscious," "near the very threshold of personality" (69-71, 73). "Crossing this threshold," however, Eswaran informs us, "is one of the most difficult tasks in the spiritual journey" (75) "You feel blocked," Easwaran professes, "by an impenetrable wall. Bodhi is a glimpse of the other side, as when you drop a quarter into the telescope near the Golden Gate Bridge and the shutter flashes open for a two-minute look at sea lions flickering on the rocks" (75). It is here that Eswaran's appropriately Golden Gate Bridge-infused description of what happens in the third dhyana, in the stage of awareness-deepening, moves nearer to the threshold of Kandel's own language, her own knowledge of the "process" of enlightenment in "Song of the Blue-Light Dakini." Alongside Easwaran's description of a seemingly "impenetrable wall" obstructing an individual's way to deeper immersion within the realm of what he (like Jung) calls the "collective unconscious," we can observe with greater contextual width the way Kandel speaks in the poem of "mountains" upon "mountains" of "substance," mountains that, like the walls of distractions, disappointments, and illusions that seek to deter our attention, must be ascended, descended through, penetrated, and transcended, if we are to truly become spiritually (or creatively) awakened.

With the spiritual context Easwaran provides, we can now also more lucidly understand the way that Kandel, with deep meditative awareness, formally and aesthetically "stills" the mind of both the speaker and the reader, placing vocal pauses or visual spaces at key moments in the poem's travel through the fields or planes of (poetic) consciousness. These pauses—these spaces, or "gaps," as Brenda Knight might call them—are what Easwaran calls "concerted" efforts to still the mind as it moves layer by layer, rung by rung, "cloud" after "flaky" cloud, out, across, down, and through realms of awareness, navigating delicately the cosmic waters of foamy thought. Interestingly, there are four key moments, four crucial "aesthetic dhyanas," or points of creative meditation, in which these gaps occur in the poem, denoted by the addition of increased blank space within the lines. Let us consider each of these stages briefly, on the way to a more replete understanding of the way that Kandel makes "the walls" between the individual and "the rest of creation" fall in "Song of the Blue-Light Dakini."

The first gap, or breath, (can we call it the space of a metric breath, a meditative in-breath?) occurs in the poem's second line, when the speaker asserts that "the substance is of a different texture." First, by pausing momentarily to allow "substance," the linguistic "substance," the disyllabic constitution of the very word "substance" itself to register in the reader's auditory consciousness, Kandel offers the reader a space to understand that there are "sub" "stance(s)," places to "stand" and "dwell" beneath the surface of the reality we perceive in everyday life and that these substances are accessible, at least initially, through the medium of language and the particularizing "telescope" of poetry. We can see this as both a sign of Kandel's own marked command over the English language and a signifier of the subterranean Beat movement itself, peering always beneath the surface of mainstream culture in search of undiscovered planes of religious thought or creative insight. Additionally, the pause after the word "substance" allows Kandel to enact her poetry of process where we watch her, through our own aesthetic telescope, performing her poetry, spontaneously, but quiescently, upon the meditative page. The blank space is a brief stillness—a resting place where Kandel jumps the gap of rational thought in order to cross the threshold into intuition where the "textures" accessible to us on the "other" side of the "mountains" are of a "different" linguistic constitution or conceptual formation. Moreover, like the Buddha, Kandel is astute to the limitations and excesses of language, what in "Emerald Poem," she more than once calls, "the point without words." She goes no further in her description of the "textures" precisely because doing so would not only diminish the wonder and necessary difficulty of our own solitary (but fulfilling) travel across the "mountains" into our own deep oceans of consciousness," but her lack of specificity about the "textures" also suggests that she herself has not quite figured out how the "textures" of consciousness might be described through the limits of human speech. For a poet, whose job, as di Prima tells us, is to "make images," this is a humble confession indeed, a wholly Buddhist one to be sure.

Furthermore, to ascribe feeling, sensation, or figures of speech to the "textures" would most certainly defeat the purpose of the meditation she is engaged in through and within the poem itself. Transcending the limitations of our senses, our various socially conditioned "likes and dislikes," Easwaran tells us, is something an enlightenment seeking individual does in the first dhyana (69). Kandel's "Blue-Light" speaker has already moved beyond that stage in her journey toward Buddhist nirvana, perhaps marking a point in her poetry where she veers from her sister-poet, di Prima, who, at least in her Zen poetry, derives spiritual awareness from sensory engagement. Kandel's Dakini is, by poem's end, three-quarters of the way to enlightenment on her poetic map beyond the barriers prohibiting spiritual awakening. Kandel's arrival at the doorstep of enlightenment at the end of the poem is therefore most certainly the result of her willingness to oscillate and undulate within the cosmic waves of an imperfect meditation, of one that, like di Prima's admittedly flawed practice of Buddhist meditation, requires both continued poise and perpetual pause for contemplation. Therefore, the pauses within the poem might also signify moments where the speaker of the poem regathers and refocuses her attention again on each poetic image at hand, each image serving as the object of her meditative concentration on the way to a wider and more sustained awareness. Consequently, when the poem's speaker announces that "some become star earth becomes cloud," in the subsequent line of the poem, the gap in between images is a signifier of a fork in which, as Frost might agree, "two roads" have "diverged" in a wood of consciousness. Once again, Kandel finds herself at the crossroads between ground and sky, earth and "cloud," faced with the spiritual and aesthetic challenges of merging the known and the unknown. Indeed, stone, over the span of many years grinds down into sandy particles, just as starlight blows out and scatters like a million particles of dust in a galaxy of intermittent darkness. In a sense though, a gradually decomposed stone's "substance," like the disintegrative image di Prima conjures of her "broken stone island" in her Preface on Kandel, is akin to the stuff of which a star is made by way of energy transferred within an atomically saturated universe. Additionally, the word "Stone," without a definite or an indefinite article to grind it into linguistic particularity, is involved, then, in the constitution and "texture" of other entities—in this case, "stars." But what do the stars become then, the speaker's pause seems to ask with an implied force? Where does their light go? Which organism will absorb the shattered light, the scattered dust, of the muted star? To such questions, the speaker provides no direct answer. Unless of course, it is the "earth," not just the earth itself, but those of us who inhabit earth, who "store" the light of stars within individual and collective memory for eternity and come to absorb that fizzled starlight (and are increased by its dissipative magnitude, its sparkles of sublimity). Perhaps it is the task of the poet, then, as Donne once suggested, to "go and catch a falling star" and transfer (and re-transmit) its energy, through poetry, within and across living memory. But if memory, for Buddhists, is, potentially, the stuff of ego and mind's reconstruction of a past that is in actuality an eternal present that is continuous experience itself, and a shifting and non-fixed "I," then poetry, Suzuki Roshi would have agreed, can be a way to propel the energy of memory—lived experience—forward, without end. Poetry can be an efficient, sustainable way to turn shared lived experience into future creative potential. If nature, by way of its own passage through the various stages of the hydrogen cycle, for instance, can turn "earth" to "cloud," (water evaporating and then falling again) then so can poetry turn "everyday experience" into a higher state of spiritual "awareness" and ecstatic consciousness where, line by "line into infinity," meditative breath by meditative breath, we can begin to see the world as if from above a shadowy "mountain," beyond an obstructive "cloud" of unknowing.

In that elevated place, a place we have ironically come to by way of descending through depths of consciousness, we begin to recognize that even "flesh becomes space," even "breath becomes time" (Kandel 8). Flesh dissolves—lives end, and bodies *do* disintegrate—

but life does not end. Our energy is "transmuted," as both Kandel and di Prima often say, the breath of our lives coming to transpire in the bodies of "others," in the inspired poems of "others." It is for this reason that "breath" ultimately becomes "time" and that the fourth syntactical gap in the poem becomes, slightly, but still significantly, the narrowest on the page in Kandel's poem. Though complete enlightenment—"total" awareness—is not achieved by poem's end (demonstrating that, to become "awake," this one poem alone is not enough) Kandel's speaker brings us to a deeper level of awareness where we realize, suddenly, that enlightenment *may* in fact be possible if we are willing to meditate long enough to experience it firsthand. Gradually, we begin to breathe along in rhythm with the universe, the way a poet breathes along with the accented or syllabic universe of his or her poem, and cross the threshold into a more continuously flowing time where we move as one with a world we have sacredly come to co-inhabit. "We slip through," as Kandel does, momentarily, at poem's "end," into a realm of deep awareness where "the waters of the collective unconscious close over [our] head[s]" (Easwaran 77). Through stillness, contemplation, poetic attention, and the poet's creative generosity, we enter briefly, if only to dip our toes (the Dakini leading us by the hand) into a "stream" that feeds into to a river of enlightenment.

"Uncompromising Enlightenment": Lenore Kandel's Quest for the "Original Energy" of "Infinite Perception(s)"

In the American spiritual tradition of di Prima, Ginsberg, H.D., Emerson, and Thoreau—all of whom, on some level, engaged the wisdom of the East— Lenore Kandel's American poetic, Eastern religious quest for personal and creative enlightenment is motivated by an impulse to follow the path of language to its far reaches, where it brings us once again into contact with what Marc Olmsted calls the "Beat Primordial Ground." In the mystic, spirit-seeking tradition of Whitman, Kandel "invites" her "soul" to enter a realm of consciousness "unchecked," replete with "original energy." Like Whitman's own dakini-like speaker in the opening verse of "Song of Myself," Kandel's poetic speakers reveal an "unabashed" willingness to celebrate the holiness of a life search for the deep interiors and far exteriors of human consciousness. With a resoundingly proto-Beat, lax intensity and vagabond electricity, many of us will recall Whitman's roaming speaker proclaiming:

> I celebrate myself, and sing myself...
> For every atom belonging to me as good belongs to you.
> I loaf and invite my soul...
> My tongue, every atom of my blood, form'd from this soil, this air...
> Hoping to cease not till death.
> I harbor for good or bad, I permit to speak at every hazard,
> Nature without check with original energy.
> (1, 3-4, 6, 9-10, 13)

While I am not supposing that Whitman's language here is *definitively* Buddhist, these sacred words, as Arthur Versluis has reminded us, read as though transmitted across a wide century from the incantatory Whitman to the mantric Kandel and her

Beat counterparts (and from the Beats to us). And now, over half a century removed from the summit of Beatdom, the poem continues to split open like an atom with fresh meaning in an age of spiritual bewilderment and religious tension such as our own. Like the "original energy" transferred between Suzuki Roshi and the Beats, like the Zen energy transmitted and exchanged through poetry between di Prima and Katagiri Roshi and like the bonds formed between di Prima and Kandel in late sixties San Francisco, the passage from Whitman confirms Kandel's belief, in "Enlightenment Poem," that we have, at one time, "all been brothers" (19). It is within the transmission of spiritual and aesthetic energy and feeling—from poet to poet and being to being—that the force of "atoms" splitting, spinning, and spouting forth with "original energy," changes hands and charges poet, reader, and poem (as di Prima, or Ray McNiece, might say) with the spirit of a deeper religiosity. These are, in fact, collective hands that reach across time and space to touch the core of aesthetic and spiritual truth. Furthermore, Whitman's imagery of a poetic, singing "tongue," "form'd" from "soil" and "air" closely resembles the very language Kandel uses in "God/Love Poem" where the speaker's "tongue" makes worship to her divine lover's body. Additionally, the lines from Whitman bear a close resemblance to the lines from di Prima's Preface where she poetically describes Kandel as simultaneously dwelling "in earth and in the middle of the air." Not coincidentally, di Prima's reading of Kandel's life and work is remembered as though through a Whitmanesque kaleidoscope of expanded consciousness where everything between ground and sky—which is to say "form'd," or *made* of heaven and earth—is fair game for spiritually and creatively-receptive American poets like Whitman, Kandel, di Prima, and Ginsberg, all of whom left their doors of perception open and their eastern windows perpetually ajar.

This deeper religiosity, this Whitmanesque attention to both the vitality of the human "form" (forming and being formed *by* poetry) and the potential for a spiritual life beyond the body, manifests itself, for both Whitman and Kandel, as a non-dual relationship between flesh and spirit intimately symbolized by Buddhist/ancient-Indian ideas about the synchronicity (not the binary opposition) that exists between the earthly and the celestial. If "Song of the Blue-Light Dakini" is Kandel's meditation on the lengths and reaches of human consciousness—her poetic foray into the depths and widths of a Buddhist "collective unconscious"—then her oft anthologized "Enlightenment Poem," is Kandel's declaration of the power of "primordial" energy of "nature without check," human life before inevitable social conditioning, before gradual cellular evolution. Moreover, the poem (which I will quote here momentarily) represents Kandel's very flirtation with creative "enlightenment," the closest contact she makes as a poet with a full artistic awakening. If "God/Love Poem" signals Kandel's move toward spiritual union through the vessel of the divine, erotic body, and if "Blue-Light Dakini" chronicles her passage through non-duality and the dissolution of ego into the realm of "bodhi," then "Enlightenment Poem" is what its title suggests it is: Kandel's closest encounter with the fourth dhyana—an unobstructed glimpse of nirvana.

Indeed, "Enlightenment Poem" confirms Kandel's very own aesthetic claim in "Poetry is Never Compromise," that truly enlightening poetry resists "compromise." It is the "manifestation/translation of a vision, an illumination, an experience" (Waldman 275). Importantly, Kandel adds, "If you compromise your vision, you become a blind prophet" (275). Neither she, nor di Prima, nor Whitman, resemble blind poets, Tiresian as they might at times appear; they are, conversely, poets who have turned eastward to face an awakening sun. With what she refers to a bit later in the Introduction as "clear sight," Kandel, in perhaps her most "prophetic," "clear," and resonant voice, begins the poem by proposing that

> we have all been brothers, hermaphroditic oysters
> bestowing our pearls carelessly
>
> no one yet had invented ownership
> nor guilt nor time
>
> we watched the seasons pass, were as crystalline as snow
> and melted gently into newer forms
> as stars spun round our heads
>
> we had not learned betrayal
>
> our selves were pearls
> irritants transmuted into luster
> and offered carelessly. (1-11)

Like Diane di Prima, a practitioner of Zen meditation, Lenore Kandel, who also sat zazen in San Francisco with Shunryu Suzuki Roshi, utilizes the space of the poem here to (re)imagine humanity in its "original" form, in its nascent stages when it began as "irritant," "hermaphroditic," "unchecked" calls that later gradually "gently melted", "into" a "newer form." In a manner characteristic both of Whitman and her fellow Beat poets Ginsberg and Waldman, whom Whitman also profoundly inspired, Kandel wields poetry as a cosmic, transtemporal "telescope," an instrument through which to view the "flickering" (Easwaran's word) and "star-spun" history of the human species unfolding across time. But unlike "Song of the Blue-Light Dakini," where the individual (human) body is a potential obstruction between the self and the world of "other bodies"—other humans, other celestial or divine forms, other textual bodies, and other "textures" of consciousness—the body in "Enlightenment Poem" plays a more integral, less inhibitive role in the speaker's ability to see with transparency the paradoxically sweeping and "flickering" transmutation of the human form. The role the body plays here, in "Enlightenment Poem," is, upon further examination, a markedly more sensual one, not altogether distinct from the role the body performs in "God/Love Poem," where it acts as an agent in the unification of lovers' souls—in the achievement of spiritual harmony across the body's "boundaries" and its seemingly impassable "threshold[s]" of flesh and skin. However, if the corporeal, enlightenment-seeking "God/Love Poem" conveys a markedly more Tantric Buddhist sensibility, then "Enlightenment Poem," in its attempt to understand the delicate origins of humankind, can be interpreted as a poem evoking a more universal Buddhism, one that speaks to a core concern at the root of each of Buddhism's branches: the quest for enlightenment *within* the bounds of temporal existence.

"Stepping out of Her Body" and "Crossing the River of Sorrow to the Other Shore": Biohistorical, Sociopolitical, Psychospiritual, Mythopoetic Implications of Kandel's "Enlightenment Poem"

As if unfolding within time like a silent film before our eyes, as if displayed in slow-motion upon the wall of a planetarium-consciousness, Kandel's "Enlightenment Poem" is a slow-motion lyric poem on the development of the human creature in all of its aspects—physical, emotional, political, spiritual, and psychological. As Kandel, herself, affirms, in her essayistic meditation, "Poetry is Never Compromise," "Enlightenment Poem" is a poem, like others she has written, that is

> concerned with all aspects of the creature and of the total universe through which he moves. The aim is toward the increase of awareness...toward clear sight, both interior and exterior...This demands honesty... sometimes joyful, sometimes painful, whether to the poet or the reader or both..... [But] It feels so good that you can step outside your private ego and share the grace of the universe. (Waldman 275)

What makes the poem an "Enlightenment Poem," is the poet's ability to "move," or "step "outside" the self and experience the dynamism of creatural existence from its earliest beginnings to the present. Not coincidentally, Kandel's "honest," "clear-seeing" and "enlightened" image of "hermaphroditic oysters" giving their "pearls" away "carelessly" amid the great tide of evolution is reminiscent of the Buddha's own experience on the night of enlightenment. "In the second watch" of the night, Eknath Easwaran tells us, Siddhartha Gautama "saw the world as if in a spotless mirror" in which there unfolded "the countless births, deaths, and rebirths of other creatures," compassion "well[ing] up with him" (95). It was this moment of illumination that allowed the Buddha to recognize that it was "ignorance," or blindness, that was the first link on the chain of human suffering (95). It is therefore with Buddha-like "awareness," poetic-clear-sightedness (not "blind prophecy") and empathy or "compassion" for the human species from its very "irritant" beginnings to its "crystalline," "lustrous" human transmutations, that Kandel's "Enlightenment Poem" unfolds like a "mirror" of creation upon the field of the page.

However "joyful" and revelatory the flickering cinema of human evolution might be, it is not without "sorrow" and a tinge of regret that Kandel's poem reveals the fact that our "original," "oyster," "energy" (as Whitman confirms) is in fact a diminished energy, a spent energy, represented by the "pearls" of wisdom, beauty, truth, and light that have inevitably (and irrevocably) been "given away" throughout the evolutionary process. It is thus in chiaroscuro that the poet ultimately paints the poem's final stanzas concluding her enlightening meditation on the growth of the contemporary human, the long and complicated evolution of the individual through space, and across time. "Offered carelessly," the speaker utters with a tone of half-lament:

>   our pearls became more precious and our sexes static
>   mutability grew a shell, we devised different languages
>   new words for new concepts, we invented alarm clocks
>   fences loyalty
>   still...even now...making a feint at communion
>   infinite perceptions
>   I remember
>   we have all been brothers
>   and offer carelessly. (12-20)

In the penultimate stanza, Kandel counterbalances her previously fervent belief in what Whitman called the "original energy" of "Nature without check," with a Buddhist critique of all the following: materialism and modern economy (monetary "pearls" becoming more and more "precious" to collective society with time), human egocentrism (the "preciousness" of each and every individual's glorified life), thwarted illusions of permanence (causing "mutability" itself to change and "grow a "static" shell"), society's various checked, conditioned, heteronormative views of the "sexes" (causing "sex," "sexuality," and gender to collectively become "static"), civilization's shrewd, divisive, taxonomic categorization of "language(s)" ("new words" and "concepts" diminishing, by way of verbal distinction, our original, unspoken bonds), Western civilization's contrived, mechanistic, and imposing "invention" of time ("alarm clocks" startling us into productivity and jolting us startlingly from a vast bed of cosmic time), civilization's construction of false boundaries to keep us from loving our neighbors (iron "fences" and stone "walls" like indestructible "mountains" between us), and, finally, the civilized world's development of the "concept" of "loyalty" (which only increases the allure of betrayal and the taboo of self-efficacy, individual autonomy and self-actualization).

Nevertheless, in spite of all that Kandel quite justly has to offer by way of spiritopoetic critique of human civilization, there is reason, "even now" (twenty or more centuries later) to make a "feint at communion," an attempt at harmony between the individual and the world that is so deeply involved in the evolution of individual and collective, creatural existence. Like the Buddha, whose own visions on the night of his "enlightenment" unfolded "infinite perceptions," vast and piercing recognitions of the interconnectivity of all life, Kandel's speaker "remembers" in her "lustrous" epiphany that "we have" indeed "all been brothers" and offer ourselves "carelessly" to one another in service of the human race, with respect for the "original energy" of compassion that we all, "even now," still carry for one another. Consequently, in the poem's final couplet, Kandel's speaker becomes almost ministerial in her tone, almost a reverend before a congregation, or an aged Buddha before a sangha of aspiring disciples. In lines that offer near-apocopated, but certainly patterned, intentional rhyme between the words "brother," "offer," and "care" (embedded phonetically in the prefix of the final adverb, "carelessly") the poet's culminating sentiments echo with deep compassion in the face of all that she has previously decried within humanity, within the confined "oyster" of the modern world. The lines therefore resonate, at the poem's end, with the spirit of a blessing bestowed upon the world.

Certainly, though, some readers may wonder why, in fact, the proto-feminist, gender-antinormative Kandel would have chosen the noun "brothers" to describe the intertwined collective body of humanity at the end of the poem, especially when writers like Brenda Knight, for instance describe Kandel, di Prima, Kyger, Waldman, and the rest of the Beat Generation women as enlightened "sisters" who shared a sacred vision of humanity. One answer to this potentially small, but significant question might be that Kandel wanted to address human race at large, choosing "brothers" as a synonym for "man" (a common colloquialism, even in the sixties) or humanity at large. Fair enough. But this might still cause critics and readers to wonder about the way in which the word "brothers" reinforces the notion of a civilization held precious like a feminine pearl within the oyster-like palm of Western man. Might it then be possible that Kandel is admitting that the language of "brotherhood," the one created by "men," is the one we must work with, the one we must learn to re-rhyme and re-construct from within the obscured ruins of human evolution? Might she herself be assuming a kind of multi-gendered identity at the poem's end, where, as the poet, she embodies feminine energy, but as the speaker (the one who voices the poem), she exudes a masculine energy? Or, at last, might it simply, but powerfully be that Kandel, who published "Enlightenment Poem" in her 1967 collection *Word Alchemy*, is adopting the language of one Martin Luther King, who, in the 1960s stood up as a kind of Buddha of America on behalf of universal "brotherhood" among all men and women, across racial and ideological bounds? Might Kandel's final remark then be suggestive of the fact that, if we wish to regain some of our "original," unprejudiced Zen energy as a species, we must learn to offer ourselves up in care to our "brothers," "remembering," like Harlem Renaissance writer, Marita Bonner, that we are not so much our brothers' "keepers" as we are the ones who help enlighten them, and then set them free from physical and mental slavery?

Seen in this light, in the "luster" of its broader racial and ideological connotations, Kandel's poem indeed becomes representative of the best of what the 1960s had to offer in the way of poetry—poetry in a climate of immense social, political, artistic, and spiritual flux. "Enlightenment Poem" reflects Kandel's yearning to "step outside the private ego and share the grace of the universe," recalling her earlier sentiment from "Poetry is Never Compromise." With striking similitude, Kandel's remark on the stepping outside the ego is reminiscent of the end of another oft anthologized 1960s Zen-American poem by James Wright, where, with renewed affection for creatural existence, and a sense of spiritual rebirth, the speaker of "A Blessing" confesses, "Suddenly I realize / That if I stepped out of my body I would break / Into blossom" (21-23). Indeed, to "step out" of bodies and egos separating us from our fellow creatures, and to cross the "threshold[s]" of racial and creatural divisiveness and personal illusion is one of the great acts a Buddhist poetics makes possible within the spiritual and political confines of American life. Wright, Kandel, and di Prima—three writers, among many in the 1960s, profoundly embraced the spirit of Walt Whitman's compassionate, energetic, and receptive democratic verse. Moreover, Beat poetry, like the poetry of the Deep Image School of which James Wright, Robert Bly, and William Stafford were part, takes on as one of its principle aims, the act of self-displacement (perhaps even self-effacement) so central to American, environmentally and spiritually- conscious poetry of the late fifties, sixties, and seventies. Kandel's poetry, like much of the poetry of the 1960s, demonstrates a deep desire to move the self aside with a shove of the poetic hand, in hopes that a selfless art may allow energetic, lustrous humanity to "break" into "pearly" "blossom" again.

Furthermore, to envision (or revision) an original "energy," as Kandel does, is to live again within the "blessing" of what Buddhists consider total freedom—a spiritual and ideological liberty that certainly does not come "free" for everyone. It is perhaps for this reason that poetry in the American Buddhist tradition so often takes on the tone and tenor of celebratory lament—a tempered celebration of a liberation that comes not without the price of human, and collective creatural, suffering, one that has its roots in the Buddha's own thinking about the nature of sentient life. This thinking clearly manifests itself in the form of a near chant in the fourteenth section of the *Dhammapada*, when the Buddha makes the following holy proclamation:

> Blessed is the birth of the Buddha, blessed is the
> teaching of the dharma, blessed is the sangha, where
> all lives in harmony.
>
> Blessed beyond measure are they who pay
> homage to those worthy of homage, to the Buddha
> and his disciples, who have gone beyond evil, shed all
> fear, and crossed the river of sorrow to the other shore.
> (Easwaran 171)

Here, the Buddha's words from Easwaran's translation of the *Dhammapada* embolden the mythopoetic and globally compassionate concerns Kandel has absorbed through a deep engagement with Buddhism and its sacred texts. If a significant effect of the Buddha's own "enlightenment," was recognizing a greater need for compassionate mindfulness in the sentient world, then Kandel's "Enlightenment Poem" is itself a response to the Buddha's great realization that a "blessed" world is itself a wider "sangha" or community where "all" attempt to "live in harmony." Also noteworthy here, is the way in which the Buddha's language, like Whitman's own, is self-celebratory, but not falsely hubristic. What the Buddha sees as "blessed" in himself is, in fact, his enlightened recognition of his own interdependent relationship to all other creatures and things. If he is indeed "blessed," then so is the "dharma"—the teaching which he is able to pass on as a result of his unanticipated and humbling enlightenment. If the dharma itself is blessed, and sacred, then so is the "sangha" which will receive the blessing of its dharmic insights and teachings. Furthermore, as indicated in the second of the two verses above, if the sangha or what Kandel might call a community of human "brothers" (and sisters) "pay homage" to each other, and to Buddha, then the possibility of "go[ing] beyond evil," (both malevolence, *and* the constricting lexical connotation of the word "evil" itself) "shed[ding] fear," and "cross[ing] the river of sorrow" to the "shore" of peace, "harmony," and increased human and environmental dignity becomes a reality with transcendent possibilities. Like the Buddha, whose language here is laden with imagery of boundary-crossing and creatural-interdependency, Kandel's "Enlightenment Poem" is devoted to the possibility that, "even now," "infinite," "communion" among living creatures is possible if we can traverse the river of "careless" inhumanity and reach the shores of "selfless" brotherhood.

Given its call to peace, and to universal brotherhood, it is no surprise that "Enlightenment Poem" was a featured poem in the December, 1966, issue of Brooklyn transplant Allen Cohen's "rainbow colored," underground newspaper, *The San Francisco Oracle*, a hip, but "dizzyingly" designed paper "combining Beat poetry and fiction with avant-garde art, articles and interviews," Steve Rubenstein reports in a May 2004 article for the *San Francisco Gate*. At the top of page 21 of that fourth issue of *The Oracle*, (page 65 in Cohen's reprinted, book length edition) the words "Enlightenment Poem" appear in an emboldened, trippy swerve of rolling capital letters creating the impression of an arch through which the reader's eye is entering as it seeks out the poem, here purposefully displayed in two diametrically opposed columns to match the coupling motif on the rest of the page's layout. The poem, here moving horizontal as opposed to the standard vertical display that appears in Kandel's 2012 *Collected Poems*, features a right column beginning with the short, but evocatively, and flowery line, "our selves were petals," perhaps to catch the reader's eye passing swiftly across the page. Below the Buddhist title "Enlightenment Poem," between two featured articles—one, on the left, titled "With Love," by Kandel herself, and the other, at right, titled "Kandel and McClure: Oracles of Love," by Lee Meyerzove—is a picture of Kandel depicted as a kind of Indian mystic priestess dressed in black. In the photo, Kandel stands upright, peering straight out through a beaded screen, the kind one might find in an Indian village in summer, or in the threshold of a doorway leading into a palm reader's shop in a 1960s San Francisco back alley. Half the beads are black and the other half pale, or gold, to match the tone of the poem's illuminating title. Kandel's hands come clasping together just below her waist, half open to the reader, as if about to form the mudra position which Zen master's like Suzuki Roshi and his students took in the Zen center not far away. Half of the poet's face (to the viewer, her left half) is all lit up; the other half is almost completely obscured and has been dissolved by a shadow. On her right wrist, one can find a few thin, silver bracelets; on the right wrist, markedly darker, thicker bracelets, of the Indian variety. Here, Cohen's photographer has depicted Kandel as a complete embodiment of "luster" and darkness, matching the paradoxical tones of joy and lament that resonate equally in "Enlightenment Poem." Also paradoxical, and seemingly incongruous, is the poet's smile, which like the Buddha's, exudes both a sense of innocence and wisdom, a sense of mischief or immense calm.

The image, like the poem, says a lot about the way in which Kandel was viewed in San Francisco throughout the 1960s. To editors like Cohen and fellow poets like di Prima, Kandel was a mythic figure who seemingly relished the opportunity to carry on this mythic persona, so long as it carried with it the deep radiance that emanated simultaneously from the heart of her poetic vision. Additionally, the photo displays a poet who has wholly embraced all that the East has "offered" the West, to use Kandel's own word. Here, in the image from *The San Francisco Oracle*, 1966, Kandel peers out of the image's uneven frame wearing the look of the enlightened poet "oracle" of the 1960s, though Ronna C. Johnson is indeed one critic who has expressed her displeasure with this female-oracle archetype weighing down a poet too dynamic to pin down in caricature. Regardless of whether Kandel helped perpetuate this mythic persona or not, both her creative authenticity, and her profound concern (like Buddha) for the well-being of sentient creatures, transcends any mythic role she may or may not have willingly played within a predominantly male-centered poetic movement such as the Beat Generation. What should strike us more, in my estimation, is the way in which Kandel's writing, even in the small feature article titled, "With Love," seems to embrace a kind of spiritual and psychic language both quintessentially 1960s and very much ahead of its time. Kandel, as if speaking both to insecure, spiritually and sexually-repressed young women and men of her generation, says with sincerity:

> You are beautiful. We are beautiful. You are divine. We are all divine. If in the secret corners of your mind you find yourself ugly and dirty and unworthy of love, it will be impossible for you to give or receive love.
>
> ...You can begin by accepting and loving yourself as a manifestation of the divine and then extending that outward. Not only through physical love, but as a generative and pervasive force directed toward all sentient beings with the hope of total consciousness and awareness for us all.
>
> ...There is only one direction to go in, and it is reached by opening the eyes into absolute clarity....With Love. (Cohen 65)

This heavily Buddhist-inflected, personal letter of sorts to the paper's readers embodies the various essences that linger in the wake of Lenore Kandel's life and serves as an all-encompassing summation of the numerous thematic concerns that pervade her poetry, both in *Word Alchemy* and beyond. Responding here in prose to Buddha himself and, perhaps, to her mentor's (Suzuki Roshi's) teachings, as well as to the charges of censorship charges brought upon her that same year after Lawrence Ferlinghetti's *City Lights Books* and Allen Cohen's *Psychedelic Shop* were raided for carrying copies of her *Love Book*, Kandel humbly, but powerfully, issues a dual call for self-realization and selflessness in the direction of her readers. To her readers, as she does in her poems, Kandel seems to scream a vital "secret" from the "corner" of her own mind, imploring people to break "through the ice that has frozen over the words of their bodies," as Lee Meyerzove eloquently says in his complementary article on that same page of *The Oracle*. Said perhaps another way, Kandel invites poets, outcasts, curious readers, and members of the Haight-Ashbury subculture to melt the "ice" of insecurity in order to share the "divine," "beauty" of our shared humanity "With love." She makes it possible for her readers, both then and now, to recognize that the power of artistic expression and political change lie within each one of us, eternally, here now.

Kali of Fierce Strength and Abiding Compassion:
The Practice of Poetic Generosity and the Transfer of Enlightened Energy from Poet to Suffering Poet

For the Beats poets, and in particular Diane di Prima and Lenore Kandel, poetry is a practice of generosity, a "generative" process, as Kandel suggests in her *Oracle* article, in which the energy that comes from self-actualization and personal liberation is diffused and "offered" up to others in a poetic ritual of fierce compassion. Di Prima and Kandel, life-long meditators and practitioners of Zen Buddhism, and later on, co-devotees of Tibetan Buddhism, place deep faith in the ways that poetry and spirituality can nurture a world in perpetual chaos and radical tumult. Now, over half a century after di Prima, Kandel, and the Beats began living and writing together, in New York, and later, in San Francisco, we readers and practitioners of peace find ourselves in need of new maps of faith in a globalized world looking more religiously pluralistic and spiritually hybridized than the world poets and spiritual practitioners inhabited in the twentieth century. Poets like di Prima and Kandel provide for us a markedly open spiritopoetic discourse with which we can begin to live and write as we quest on, out into the tenuous landscape of twenty-first century religion and art.

In the geospiritually confounding era in which we live, we can look to the works of Lenore Kandel and Diane di Prima as vehicles of receptivity in an age of constricted compassion, remembering that our wars over resources and our quests for monetary power are the very causes of our collective spiritual ignorance and civic discord. Like the generous pluralism exuded by the literature of the Harlem Renaissance, Beat literature, Stephen Prothero reminds us, "concern[s] itself with spiritual emancipation and the cultivation of a vast view, a Big Sky Mind" (13). With a piercing vision, and an incantatory tone, Kandel reminds us, in another poem from *Word Alchemy*, titled "Vision of the Skull of the Prophet," that

> in the moment of shattering the prophet eye
> views the entire universe
> and dies again to dust
>
> at the moment of sight
> any being can share the total vision
> any being whose eyes at that incalculable instant
> are completely open (10-16)

Like di Prima, for whom the "moment of sight," the experience of "darshan," is vital to the illumination of truth and the recognition of harmony among living creatures, Kandel's prophet's "eye," is, in a sense, the eye of the "universe" itself widening its "entire," "vision" much the way Emerson's "transparent eyeball" is for transcendentalists, a potent symbol of omniscient sight. Kandel's own primordial "vision" of the prophet's skull is the poet's way of holding within her imagination the skull of a fragile world that exists always on the verge of "shattering." But it is precisely the poet's recognition of universal fragility, of the fact that all things in the universe inevitably die "again to dust," that makes her statement more prophetic. To live on the threshold between "totality" and impermanence, as both di Prima and Kandel do, is to live "completely open," in Buddhist fashion, within each instantaneously beautiful and terrible moment of universal creation, with its unending pattern of life springing-up and life whittling-down.

For Buddhist poets, di Prima and Kandel, the "total" universe is an expansive page upon which out-breaths and-breaths manifest in a discourse of sacred, creative energy. Moreover, both di Prima's contractive, taut, Zen verse, and Kandel's sweeping, elastic poetry of breath are written, through Buddhist mindfulness and compassion, into being. Upon the open page of experience where their respective poems are written, "the ego goes out of the work in favor of the oneness, the small self dissolve[ing] into the large self" (the" big mind") "of all life" (Smith 13). As the title of Larry Smith's Introductory Essay in *America Zen* suggests, Kandel and di Prima live and write "Outside the Box" of conditioned thought and "Inside the Circle" of "total" creation. Their poetry is in fact energized by the spirit of creation, by the very electricity of a life teeming with perpetual receptivity, which Kandel exhibits in "Joy Song," when she suddenly realizes

> What a pleasure to be a honey plant
> and
> open wide. (4-6)

Once again, without the final, punctuating period, Kandel's lines from *Word Alchemy* reflect a poet who is "open wide," completely receptive to the sweet, erotic wisdom of insecurity. Like di Prima, the imperfect meditator, Kandel is a poet continually in the midst of a process, a "plant" in mid-growth offering the "honey" of language and the "honeysuckle" of her own creative body (as she does in "God/Love Poem") to a world that needs art as a form of love and healing, as a means of imaginative and spiritual sustenance in a century running low on spiritual and emotional resources.

There is perhaps no poem more demonstrative of Kandel's credo that poetry is an uncompromising force of spiritual sustenance and creatural preservation than her poem "Small Prayer for Falling Angels." With a voice of compassion and sheer honesty, the speaker of Kandel's poem, now increasingly vulnerable, and spiritually "open wide," confesses:

> too many of my friends are junkies
> too many of my psychic kin tattoo invisible revelations
> on themselves
> singing their manifestoes to etheric consciousness with
> little
> hoofprint scars reaching from fingertip to fingertip
> a gory religiosity akin to Kali's sacred necklace of fifty
> human heads
>
> Kali-Ma, Kali-Mother, Kali-Ma, Kali-Mother
> too many of my friends are running out of blood,
> their veins
> are collapsing it takes them half an hour to get a hit
> their blood whispers through their bodies, singing its
> own death chant
> in a voice of fire, in a voice of glaciers, in a voice of sand
> the ash blows
> forever
> over emptiness. (1-12)

The inciting quintet of "Small Prayer," with its *medias res* opening and its characteristically dynamite bursts of Beat word formation, coupled with the reverential softness and meditative rhetoric of the subsequent septet combine to produce a paradoxically sonorous quiet in Kandel's spiritual ode to her wounded, fellow Beat pilgrims. The poem's rolling-stone-thrust, nowhere more exhibitive than in the poem's second and third lines, where the speaker, in Ginsbergian fashion, tells us that "too many" of her drug-tripping, road-tripping "psychic kin" tattoo invisible revelations on themselves / singing their manifestoes to etheric consciousness." Through the use of verbal paradox here, Kandel evokes an image of Beat-poet-junkies who metaphorically "tattoo" or imprint their spirits and psyches with the "revelatory" language and beliefs of a more "ethereal" Eastern "consciousness." "Singing" their "manifestoes" of far consciousness aloud in the American night, these "howling" Buddhist, celestial, starry-dynamo dwellers bare the "hoofprint scars" of a "gory religiosity" akin to the many-skulled, "divine," Hindu mother goddess Kali, "the black one," the dark but shimmering Beat saint of awareness who is the "consort" of fiery "Shiva" (Friedrichs 170). Kandel thus calls on Kali here to heal the "scars" of a wounded generation whose bodies and spirits are burning out like "stars" in what Ginsberg, in "Howl," famously called the alienating "machinery of night."

If, therefore, the first stanza of Kandel's "Small," religiously ambiguous or universal invocation of "Kali," is what its title suggests—a "Prayer" for the diminishing health of poets who have done as much physical harm to themselves as they have artistic good for poetry at large—then the poem's second stanza marks a distinctly *Buddhist* turn in the poem's spiritual atmosphere. In stanza two, the poet calls upon the fierce, (even violent) but compassionate *Hindu* "Mother," Kali, so that she may "forever" protect the body and "blood" of her "friends." The poem's second stanza is a particularly crucial one in the way that it not only reveals Kandel's deep familiarity with the religion and lore of the East, but it is also reflective of a greater religious pluralism that pervades the writing of the Beat Generation. Within the potentially Christian-resonant image of poet-"angels" "falling" through/in/from a Western (American/Californian) sky, and within an over-arching Buddhist ethos of compassion and a Zen "Prayer" for eternal "emptiness," Kandel casts her Hindu Kali as an agent of thunderous peace and rumbling maternity. Through the agonized songs of "fire," "glacier(s)," and fierce "wind," only Kali, the divine mother who dances along with Shiva to the cosmic shuffle of life and death, is capable of saving these "revelatory" "junkies" from "collapsing" and "falling" to their howling, harrowing deaths. "As the Divine Mother," Kurt Friedrichs informs us, Kali "destroys ignorance, maintains the world order, and blesses and frees those who strive for the knowledge of God. Kali is therefore the symbol of dissolution and destruction" (170). Seen in the light of Friedrichs' description of Kali, Kandel's "Small Prayer for Falling Angels" takes on a deeper significance—a vaster, and more sweeping and inclusive spiritual light. If, indeed, Kali symbolizes awareness, universal "order," spiritual freedom, along with "dissolution" and "destruction" then Kali, one might say, is the paradoxical patron saint of the Beat Generation. She signifies, both for Kandel, and her readers, all that Beat poetry embodies in the way of violent creativity, volatile sensitivity, and turbulent compassion. However, like the Buddha, Kali is also, for Beat poets, not a figure of extremes or polarities, but a beacon of universal nuance and creatural intricacy. Her very being defies conformity and philosophical categorization, containing within her "divine" presence a plethora of Whitmanesque "multitudes" beyond good and evil.

With this contextual understanding of Kali in mind, let us pause here for a moment before hearing the concluding stanzas of "Small Prayer for Falling Angels," to consider what Kandel might have drawing upon for her image of "Kali-Ma," protector of all Beat poets "falling" mercilessly through society's cracks in "Blake-light tragedy," to borrow a phrase from Ginsberg. Given the multiple appearances of her own poems in its tripped-out pages, and her own participation in San Francisco's artistic subculture and its culture of Zen awareness, it is highly likely that Kandel, whose poem to Kali-Ma appeared in print in 1967, came across Bob Branaman's neon-pink and blue depiction of "Kali" in the August, 1967, issues of Cohen's *San Francisco Oracle*, his illustration featured in the ninth issue of the two year paper.

Figure 1:
Kali, by Bob Branaman,
San Francisco Oracle,
August, 1967

Branaman's "Kali," like Kandel's, is depicted here as a defender of creation and a protector of humanity, evidenced by the wide, all-encompassing shield that occupies the center of the goddess' body. In fact, Branaman's intentional decision to make the shield the very middle part of Kali's body is highly emblematic of a Beat poetic and artistic vision of the body as a fortification around the spirit, the body itself as much an agent of spiritual protection against mainstream culture's assault on the human being. Additionally, Branaman's multi-circular shield—signifying here a world in which suffering has no beginning, and no end—reflects the spinning, and seemingly interminable repetition which Kandel employs in the poem's second stanza as she repeats the phrase of "Kali-Mother, Kali-Ma" two times in a single line, chanting in an almost tribal fashion, the way her friends' "blood" makes its own "death chant" as it runs out of those poets' fragile lives. Kandel's poem therefore mirrors Branaman's illustration of suffering, shield-dwelling figures spinning forth, in the way it principally seeks to evoke the vision of inherent suffering that compromises Buddhism's first noble truth. Both Kandel and Branaman are aware of the reality that suffering exists, and that suffering itself is embedded within each repeated act of creation. This is no more evident than in the shield that forms the spirit-center of Kali's body in Branaman's illustration. The shield itself is like the samsaric round of life and death spinning incessantly at the center of the drawing and at the nucleus of sentient life.

What distinguishes Branaman's illustration from Kandel's poem, however, is the markedly light and almost whimsical feeling it invokes in the viewer. Whereas Kandel's poem conveys a "gory," almost nightmarish vision of contemporary poetic life—one where poets are literally dying for a "fix" that will transport them from the spiritual disappointment and cultural apathy they experience in a country which continues to send soldiers off to war in spite of the fact that they continue to "fall" like "angels" in the jungles of Vietnam. Though the title of the issue in which Branaman's artwork appears is in fact titled, "Psychedelics, Flowers, and War," his Kali—holding up in her right hand a "flower" of peace amid the psychedelic, spiritual-neon field of the illustration—is, compared with Kandel's poem, much less demonstrative of the kind of *inner* war going on within poets and civilians of San Francisco's, and America's, late 1960s. Moreover, whereas Branaman's Kali stands alone in isolation, far-removed from the small temple from which she has ostensibly emerged at the bottom left of the illustration, Kandel's poem paints a picture of a collective generation awaiting a goddess' arrival from within the ruined temple of their own desperation. If Branaman's electric pink and powder blue Kali can be said to signify the artist's sense that exuberance and peace can be quickly kindled again within *The Oracle*'s iridescent pages, then Kandel's poem, never printed in *The Oracle*, might more closely resemble an expressionist painting depicting a deeper psychic suffering, one rendered in fierce, haunting crimson, and stark, harrowing black.

Keeping in mind what Brenda Knight has called Kandel's "voracious" reading habits and her "vast" knowledge within the fields of comparative religion and mythology, it is fair to suppose that Kandel may have drawn her own image of Kali from more than Branaman's illustration alone (279). Acquainted as she seems to have been with Buddhist and Hindu sculpture, imagery, and iconography, Kandel would have more than likely been familiar with the eleventh to thirteenth century Indian sculpture of Auspicious Kali depicted below, in which a four-armed Kali seated (perhaps upon a small casket) feet pressed delicately down upon the cosmic world, is holding up for the viewer, not a flower of peace, but instead various symbols of suffering, birth, and death—images of creation and destruction that pervade human existence. Might the upper right arm holding a small noose serve here as a symbolic recognition Kandel herself made in verse of the stranglehold that suffering has over humanity? Might this Indian Kali's noose be indicative of a world plagued by mental and physical slavery, and might her small trident, depicted in her lower left hand, signify a weapon with which to break that slavery?

Figure 2:
Ritual Trident with the Hindu Deity, Auspicious Kali

If we glance quickly at the sculpture for a moment, the trident might almost be mistaken for a writing implement, an implement with which art strives to break the noose of suffering and moral entrapment. The imaginative Kandel could have easily conceived of Auspicious Kali in this way when she first saw the bronze sculpture of the goddess exhibited in '63 or '64, after it was purchased and then donated to the Asian Art Museum in San Francisco by Chicago Avery Bundage in 1962 (Asian Art Museum Curatorial Department).

Considering the degree to which physical enslavement, lynching, and chaining pervades American literature, and American history at large, and considering the way that Beat writing is consumed with images of separation from and transcendence beyond societal constriction, the above image of Kali is therefore a particularly potent one in the way it encapsulates a core concern of American writing. Seen in light of the Asian Art Museum's bronze sculpture, Kali comes, in a sense, to represent the work of twentieth century Buddhist female (and perhaps even male) writers penning their way out of moral and physical oppression. Moreover, the eleventh century Kali emboldens American Buddhist literature (simultaneously accented by Hinduism) in a couple of prominent ways. For one thing, the sculpture above affirms that Eastern spiritual modes of depicting suffering were indeed on the American minds, enough for them to graft their way into American poetic and narrative consciousness. Additionally, they serve as iconographic manifestations of complex American attitudes about moral depravity, personal suffering, and intense ethical and spiritual doubts about American society and Western Civilization at large. Indeed, di Prima and Kandel appear to have their fingers on the pulses of numerous contemporary spiritual and cultural issues, and subsequently look east in search of various complex and nuanced aesthetic answers to bewildering national and global dilemmas.

The Indian sculpture of Kali is significant to our understanding of Kandel's poem, and to our contextual understanding of American Buddhist literature in yet one more way. Despite the fact that it is less playful than Branaman's American illustration of Kali, Auspicious Kali is still more serene and less menacing than some of the other depictions of Kali that we encounter throughout Eastern sculptural and pictorial history. Indeed, the image depicted above is a markedly more ambiguous goddess, a more tenuous figure who, like Kandel herself, seems to stand (or sit) on the threshold of what Yeats called a "terrible beauty." Open and receptive to the viewer, sitting with her suffering as she looks out across the far reaches of human time, *this* Kali confirms, as Wallace Stevens believes, that "death is the mother of beauty." Moreover, like Buddha Calling Earth to Witness, Kali-Ma calls *us* here, as she does in Kandel's poem, delicately, and perhaps even a tad reluctantly, to witness the inscrutable bond between life and death, pain and joy, suffering and healing, destruction and creation. With an upper left hand that cautions us, like Buddha's, but also pushes threat away from our lives, Kali herself is like Kandel, holding back the kinetic thrust of suffering as it advances in the direction of the world's wounded poets. With her bottom right hand, Kali holds a bowl shaped like an open skull, within which lies the invisible water of a purer eternity.

It is thus in the water of a purer poetic stream, that Kandel, a spokesperson for the goddess in a world that needs the goddess' healing power, bathes language in the final stanzas of "Small Prayer for Falling Angels," calling on Kali in a litany of sonic blessings. With relentless anaphoric lines of unforced breath, the poem's speaker chants:

> Kali-Ma, remember the giving of life as well as the
> giving of death
>   Kali-Ma...
> Kali-Ma, remember the desire is for enlightenment and
> not oblivion
>   Kali-Ma...
> Kali-Ma, their bones are growing light, help them to fly
> Kali-Ma, their eyes burn with the pain of fire; help them
> that they see
> with clear sight
> Kali-Ma, their blood sings death to them; remind them
> of life
> that they be born once more
> that they slide bloody through the gates of yes, that
> they relax their hands nor try to stop the movement of
> the flowing now
> too many of my friends have fallen into the white heat of
> the only flame
> may they fly higher, may there be no end to flight.
> (13-25)

In the final stanzas of "Small Prayer for Falling Angels," the often erotic, often politically retaliatory, often feminist-revisionist Kandel is at her most compassionate, her most intimately connected with the world she inhabits—a world comprised of the very forces of "life," "death," and the enlightenment that arises as a result of their inevitable collision. For Kandel, a Buddhist poet operating not within, but beyond, the poles of good and evil, the "desire" is neither moral edification nor political correctness, but instead, absolute commitment to a path of "enlightenment" found behind the golden "gates of yes" where "eyes that burn with the pain of fire" and mortal suffering can once again be blessed with the waters of "clear sight." Like the eleventh century sculpture of Kali, Kandel's "Kali-Ma" is protector, destroyer, creator, and healer all at once. Like the Kali depicted in the Indian sculpture, Kandel's Kali can help those who worship her "take flight" from harm. Like the poets whose "blood sings death to them," those who view Branaman's "Kali," the eleventh century Indian sculpture of Kali, and the sculpture of the *Buddha Calling Earth to Witness*, for that matter, can be "reminded of life" (as Kandel is, as we are) and "be born once more," not into the round of samsara, (as interminably circuitous as Branaman's Kali's shield) but into a life, an awakened state, where nirvana can at last be attained. In such a realm, in such a life—a life to be experienced here and now—human "bones" can "grow light," not heavy and withered with suffering. Instead, replete with "luster," and immense emerald luminosity, the poet's bones can be lit up again with breath and creative vitality. Like Kali's serene eleventh century face and the upper left hand she holds up with grace as if to calm chaos and bring order to tumult, Kandel's poem is an attempt to restore life, beauty, and dignity to a generation of poets who "slid" dangerously close to death, some, even, whom entered its "gates" and did not return. For the latter, this "Small Prayer" is an attempt to give them "wings" with which to fly high beyond the "white heat" of delusion and hellish death's all-encompassing "flame." For these poet-junkies, Kali is the sacred "dakini" the poet chooses to guide them out of "oblivion," suffering, and endless neglect.

Conclusion: Poetry Once "Trapped in Amber," Emerald Spirit Set Free—Rediscovering Lenore Kandel

In a segment of the interview titled "Fast Speaking Woman," reprinted in *Break the Rule of Cool: Interviewing and Reading Women Beat Writers*, Beat scholar Ronna Johnson shares with Beat poet Anne Waldman the feeling of surprise she encountered when she discovered a few of Lenore Kandel's poems in Waldman's anthology, *The Beat Book*. Concerning Kandel's inclusion in the anthology, the two partake in the following telling exchange of insights:

> Ronna Johnson: Getting her in there was a real coup. She's almost invisible.
>
> Anne Waldman: It's heartening that she [Kandel] resurfaced in San Francisco a few years back in time for the book fair when [Brenda Knight's] *Women of the Beat Generation* came out. A recluse now, I gather. What does she remind me of? She's Ur-feminist, radical. Her work seems trapped in amber at times. (261)

The above exchange, straight-forward as it may initially

appear, is a concise encapsulation of the difficulties one confronts in conducting serious, scholarly work on a poet like Lenore Kandel. How many of us have ever encountered Lenore Kandel's work in anthologies of "Best Loved American Poetry" or on college syllabi in Contemporary American Poetry classes? How many of us, familiar as we are with the mystique surrounding the Beat Generation, have encountered Kandel's name in a list of famous Beat writers' names like Kerouac, Ginsberg, Burroughs, Corso, or Snyder? Sometimes such lists even include popular, but still peripheral figures, like Charles Bukowski, Norman Mailer, and even Bob Dylan. Admittedly, I myself had never heard of Lenore Kandel until a professor, curious about my work on Beat poetry, suggested I investigate her poetry. When, a couple of weeks later, I received my copy of *The Collected Poems of Lenore Kandel*, and began slowly turning its illuminating pages, I soon realized that I had made a significant oversight, as many others have as well. "Trapped" in history's faded "amber" glow, the poetry of Lenore Kandel had indeed been "invisible" to me—and to other respected professors and scholars outside the Beat nexus. Nevertheless, as I read page upon page of Kandel's poetry in the July afternoon heat of my mother's empty Brooklyn apartment, Kandel's poetry, shimmering within the pages of its vibrant red dust jacket, began speaking back to me, much the way that di Prima's had, from within the silent undercurrent of America's vocally expressive, spiritually, and artistically experimental 1960s.

What I soon discovered (or, I should say, re-discovered, because, to her late fifties and sixties peers, the "legendary" Kandel was one of the leading figures of the Beat Generation) was that Lenore Kandel's Buddhist poetry, "trapped" as it may have been in the "amber" light of a gleaming moment in American literary history, is conversely anything but "trapped" in terms of its spiritual vision and its aesthetic trajectory. Kandel's poetry, as we have seen in the preceding pages, is a poetry that omits nothing from its cosmos of threshold-crossing artistic possibilities. Embracing her own teacher's, Shunryu Suzuki's, Zen praxis and its seemingly limitless and clear big minded experience of a more universal and harmonious reality, Kandel proves herself as someone who, poem after poem, sings open the gates of mystery for us so that we may experience the emerald and "blue-light" of our own spiritual and personal awakening. As noted earlier, poetry, for Lenore Kandel, is a "manifestation" of a "vision," an "illumination, an "experience." For Kandel, writing poetry is a sacred ritual-unveiling of buried truth, just as it is for her poet counterpart, Diane di Prima. And yet, paradoxically, it is also a place where one "shelters" or harbors the sacred to keep it from losing its radiant "luster" and "original energy" undiminished by global warfare and erosive time. (Kandel's poetry and home literally were sacred "shelter" for the vagabond di Prima when she stayed with Kandel in the summer of '68). Moreover, poetry, for this spontaneous Beat poet, is a sanctuary or a haven of authenticity, where undeniably terrible beauties can manifest themselves without "compromise," without conforming, as Kandel insists, to the conventions of mainstream society and its expectations of a life dualistically and all-too-easily conceived.

Time and again, in her *Love Book*, in *Word Alchemy*, and in her still largely unrecognized, unpublished poetry, Kandel embraces and embodies the spiritual and aesthetic virtues that Zen Buddhism has bequeathed to American Poetry, and in particular, to Beat poets seeking out the glistening heart of aesthetic truth "lying latent" in the deep and elusive core of emerald consciousness. With a vast spiritual willingness to let the world in, to let life flow through her very body and spirit, not altogether unlike Sufi Poets Rumi and Hafiz, and certainly, to a large degree, Buddha himself, Kandel's poetry reflects the insights of her own teacher, who in his lectures at the San Francisco Zen Center, reminded students that

> We say our [spiritual] practice should be without gaining ideas, without any expectations, even of enlightenment. This does not mean however, just to sit [Zazen] without any purpose. This practice free from gaining ideas is based on the Prajna Paramita Sutra. However, if you are not careful, the sutra itself will give you a gaining idea. It says, "Form is emptiness and emptiness is form."
> But if you attach to that statement, you are liable to be involved in dualistic ideas; here is you, form, and here is emptiness, which you are trying to realize through your form. So, "form is emptiness and emptiness is form," is still dualistic. But fortunately our [Zen] teaching goes on to say, "Form is form and emptiness is emptiness." Here there is no dualism. (Suzuki 25)

Here, in this central passage from Shunryu Suzuki's lecture "No Dualism," we can hear the ways in which Zen Buddhism has allowed Lenore Kandel to transcend, as she might say, the falsely exclusive "barriers" between "form" and "emptiness," or, as poets might perceive it, "artistic craft" and "spiritual and conceptual vision." Whereas a poet like Williams, or even Pound for that matter, might have absorbed from Japanese Zen aesthetics, the notion that, in art, there ought to exist "no ideas but in things" (as di Prima would at least half agree), Lenore Kandel's poetry reflects a more mature and thorough poetic *and* philosophical understanding of what Zen Buddhism has brought to American theories of aesthetics. While, indeed, vesting one's artistic faith in "formed," "things," as Pound, Williams, and H.D. did (all of whom were unquestionably influential on Beat poetry, to be sure), Kandel's ability to allow "form"—what we might call "objectivity," and emptiness, what we might here call "subjectivity," or subjective, nondual, vast mind—to *coexist*, is emblematic of one Zen-Romantic-Beat poet's desire to produce a fluid, porous, and dynamically shifting "body" of poetry beyond duality. Therefore, while Kandel's multi-spiritual, pluralistically-faithed poetry of the sixties is layered with imagery from Tantric, Tibetan, Hindu, and even Christian/Biblical traditions, it is Zen Buddhism's belief that "the original teaching of Buddha includes all of the various schools" that motivates Lenore Kandel's receptive poetic vision (117). "As Buddhists," Kandel seems to agree with her Zen teacher, "our traditional effort should be like Buddha's; we should not attach to any particular school or doctrine" (117).

What distinguishes Lenore Kandel's aesthetic project, therefore, is the paradoxical fact that, in spite of the vast knowledge she possesses of eastern religious traditions (holding, as she does, di Prima tells us, the "glass keys" to open wisdom's "gates") she refuses to "attach to any particular school or doctrine" within the wide open field of her "shapely," but fluid/un-fixed poetry (to recall both Duncan and Olson). For as she ecstatically discovers in her own "Emerald Poem," from the collection *Word Alchemy*:

> the solid becomes the liquid and I the greenbreather
> I am at home among the nebulae
> > in the heart of the emerald
> > safe in a point without words
> one is one and I the green breather
> > I the gill singer
> Of the liquid green flowers that the small birds carry.
> (7-13)

Once again, within the unpunctuated, porous liquidity of her non-dualistic verse, Kandel distills here, in this near *ars poetica*, the very nature of her Buddhist-poetic craft. For in Kandel's "emerald," "green" and "blue-light" poetry, this sixties dakini is the force behind a malleable "word alchemy," one where her "green," fertile poetic "breath" is the fire that melts "solid form" down to "liquid" emptiness comprised of fluid artistic, spiritual, and alchemically "dynamic" combinative, elemental constituencies. What's more, these alchemized constituencies of poetry and faith are joined in Kandel's Zen "big mind" which is, indelibly, always "at home among the nebulae," but never forgetful of the "primordial," consecrated ground to which poetry and Buddhism also belong. For Kandel then, poetry is, in fact, a non-exclusive union of charged forces—a kinetic "marriage of heaven and hell"—what Blake would have called "progression" by way of "contrariness"— where "ground" and "air," "lover" and "demon," "liquid" vision and "solid" verse are fluidly entwined like the complementary energies expressed by Lao Tzu in the *Tao Te Ching*. Finally, and paradoxically, Kandel is "safe" in the Zen/Taoist "point without words" precisely because she is aware, as Suzuki is, of the limits of speech, in language's ability to articulate an eternal truth which perhaps cannot be spoken. It is for this reason, that Kandel fancies herself not a poet with false bravado and a hubristic command over her own language; conversely, Kandel—who in truth does command language as potently as her Beat counterparts, Ginsberg and Kerouac—is content being the "gill singer," the one who pronounces a poetry of clear "breath." Like the fish breathing fresh air through its aquatic gills, Kandel takes in the Zen breath of poetry and exhales it back into the world in the form of a verse-breath conceived in measured lines of parallel suffering, and joy. With her Zen voice simultaneously firm and smooth as the "gill" of the respiring fish, she can sing her "liquid green" lotus "flowers" of images into "etheric" air like "small birds" carrying a message of faith amid the nebulous contemporary world, off to the far-reaches of poetic consciousness, where we wait at the gates of enlightenment to receive them, here, beneath starlit "mountains," ready to be made aware.

CONCLUSION

Rugged Road, Open Hand, Swinging Door

Essences of an American Beat Buddhist Poetics and the Mantra of a New Generation

An eager Buddhist aspirant once asked Master Taewon, one of Korea's well-respected living Zen teachers, "How should I follow a rugged road?" To this question, Taewon offered only a two-word answer: "Go straight" (Haight 19). While this kind of curt but seemingly esoteric retort is not uncommon to the rhetoric of Zen, the short koanistic reply speaks, in an uncannily direct way, to the spiritual path taken by Beat Generation poets of the fifties, sixties, and early seventies. If nothing else, Master Taewon's response to the aspirant is indicative of a quintessentially Buddhist belief in the undeniable reality of existential hardship, this life's inherent ruggedness. As the First Noble Truth suggests, there is in fact something of inherent nobility in realizing the real presence of our collective human fragility and receiving the wisdom that comes from a willingness to proceed "straight" along life's turbulent and seemingly unforgiving road. Seen in the light of the brief Zen dialogue between Taewon and the aspirant, life begins to take on the dual character of a potentially painful, but revelatory foray into the unforeseen provinces of our tumultuous, yet imaginative interior landscapes. From this Zen perspective, life takes on the demeanor of a rugged, yet "necessary" encounter (as Diane di Prima might say) with an inner life unfolding along the stone-flecked, dust-blown, road toward human awakening.

Along a westbound road, leading to a Far East of the mind, writers like Jack Kerouac, Allen Ginsberg, Gary Snyder, Diane di Prima, Lenore Kandel, and a host of noble others traveled in search of artistic freedom, political autonomy, and liberation from social constriction, making California, and not so distant Asia, nexuses of vast artistic potentiality in the years following WWII, and spanning the Vietnam War. Above all, their travels "on the road" allowed these Beat writers to cultivate a spontaneous, but serious spiritual life that ultimately engendered a rugged, but still elegant, Zen-suffused poetic corpus—one that has fundamentally permeated the core of American literature and culture of the late twentieth and early twenty-first centuries. Years before the outgrowth of mindfulness programs, meditation centers, and yoga studios that now populate towns and cities from coast to coast, Diane di Prima and Lenore Kandel were sitting meditatively with Japan's Shunryu Suzuki Roshi in San Francisco's first Zen centers and meditation halls. Indeed, years before Zen became a commonplace adjective or noun (or even a verb) within the linguistic cradle of our hybridizing American vernacular, di Prima and Kandel, the two transplanted New York poets, took a "Road" that "led only from Vision to further Vision" of what Zen had to offer two curious young women looking for a little lotus awareness out West (di Prima xiv). Yet, unlike the literary, spiritual "road" Kerouac was "on" and admittedly helped pave, the road di Prima and Kandel traveled in the sixties neither intersected directly with the mainstream media's "Beat-hype," nor followed the exact course paved by Kerouac-crazed college students seeking quickly-conceived alternatives to the perplexing, apparent non-complexity of suburban, American life.

In contrast to both their more vocal male poetic counterparts, and to the throngs of boisterous, bewildered hipsters and loafing dharma bums of their age, Kandel and di Prima settled down in San Francisco where, in addition to engaging in artistic and social activism, they waged a quiet revolution of the Zen interior. Here, in San Francisco, deeply invested in their own imperfect, but eclaircizing meditation(s), di Prima and Kandel struggled with the mudra position and labored to control their Zen backs and Zen breaths; however, through the process of this spiritual labor, this rugged zazen, they consequently learned the limits and potentialities of their own lyric cadences, the tones and timbers of their own breathy, bardic voices, and the spatial contours and formal dimensions of their spiritualized free-verse poems. Thus, for these Zen-minded poets, when their teacher, Suzuki Roshi, spoke to them on the importance of controlling their breathing, both on and off the mat, it was with a double-entendre (as poets and practitioners) that they were processing what the Roshi had to say about the inhalation and exhalation of meditative breath. In their listening ears, their open hands, and their "beginner's minds," di Prima and Kandel were hearing, receiving, and processing Suzuki's axiomatic assertions that

> When we practice Zazen, our mind always follows our breathing. When we inhale, the air comes into the inner world. When we exhale, the air goes out to the outer world. The inner world is limitless, and the outer world is also limitless. We say "inner world" or "outer world," but actually there is just one whole world. In this limitless world, our throat is like a swinging door. The air comes in and goes out like someone passing through a swinging door. If you think, "I breathe," the "I" is just extra. There is no you to say "I." What we call "I" is just a swinging door which moves when we inhale and when we exhale. It just moves; that is all.... To be aware of this movement does not mean to be aware of your small self, but rather of your universal nature, or Buddha nature.
> (11–12)

In a number of revelatory ways, this verbally austere, yet conceptually provocative passage from *Zen Mind, Beginner's Mind*, encapsulates the shared, deeply breathed, Buddhist, Beat poetics of Diane di Prima and Lenore Kandel. For deep at the seemingly wrought core of their rugged, Pound-and-Whitman-inspired, free-verse spiritopoeia, there lies a perpetual machine of breath which ceases to simultaneously inhale the breath of their literary and spiritual ancestry and exhale the unique, fresh out-breath of a new American, Buddhist-poetic consciousness. This poetics, like Roshi's Zen praxis, can ultimately be characterized as a poetry of the steady, but perpetually-dynamic, fluxing, "swinging door." In a Zen, "swinging-door-poetics" like the one embodied by di Prima and Kandel, time, space, breath, sound, silence, mortality, vivacity, opacity, lucidity animosity, and compassion flow endlessly and synchronously though the poets' interdependent creative anatomies of mind, heart, spirit, eye, ear, hand, and "throat" to produce a corpus of writing where each poem becomes (as I've intimated earlier) a kind of ritual of "celebratory lament." In a Buddhist, Beat poetics of celebratory lament, sorrow becomes a force of poetic generativity—an acceptance, or even an embrace, of life's creative ruggedness. Therefore, in the sorrowful felicity of many Beat, spiritual lyrics, a plunge into the waters of collective suffering serves to engender an "infinite ether" of poetic possibilities (as Kandel might say) where the poem emanates a jagged but shimmering reflection of a life broken open to absorb unforeseen human beauties.

In a sense, the poetics of the "swinging door" carries with it an inherent belief in the power of verbal simplicity and rhetorical directness—a willingness to see things and say things as they are without over-emphasizing the autonomy of the speaker's subjectivity, recognizing always the limitations of the singer's mouth, and eye's/I's capacity to see. In the poetry of the door swinging perpetually open—which we can now safely call the poetry of Diane di Prima and Lenore Kandel—a wounded, fractured world once again becomes "whole," embracing the Buddha's own aspiration of an enlightening wholeness in which one attains Buddha-nature by becoming immersed in, and harmonious with the world and by receiving and then continually offering up one's sacred artistic, human gifts to one's universal coinhabitants. Hence, the swinging, dynamic poetics of the opening door, the opening road, the opening hand, for these Beat women on the edge of suffering and the fringe of joy, is a poetics of capaciousness where the self is a site of vulnerability made accessible for the human reader's own explorations of spiritual possibility and artistic discovery. For as Buddha himself has reminded a sangha of poets, readers, singers, writers, pacifists, and aspirants:

>Those closed off from generosity
>Do not enter the realm of the gods,
>Fools do not praise generosity.
>The wise rejoice in generosity
>And by that will be happy after death.
>Better than lordship over all the worlds
>Is the fruition of the streamwinner's path. (Maitreya 49)

Seen in the light of Buddha's insights into the importance of generosity, we are able to more fully recognize the degree to which di Prima and Kandel were cultivating a poetics of selflessness that made it possible for female (and male) writers after them to join them on the "streamwinner's" (or enlightenment acquirer's) "path" to "personal and creative fruition." Like Buddha, who left his teachings behind as a source of spiritual guidance and human inspiration—as a sacred offering to be "inhaled" and then subsequently exhaled by future followers of the dharma—di Prima and Kandel, in their selfless, compassionate poems to deceased children, teachers, loved ones, friends, fallen poets, celebrated living poets, nature's creatures, lost planets, heavens, and burning stars, offer up their open hands and open-verse lines to inspire, disrupt, rejuvenate, heal, or praise a universe of sentient beings living on the threshold of awakening. Time and again, in poems like di Prima's "Song for Baby-O Unborn" and Kandel's "Small Prayer for Fallen Angels," di Prima and Kandel demonstrate an uncanny capacity for literary intimacy in the face of life's inherent transience, and in doing so, certify that, indeed, one of the principle vocations of the contemporary Buddhist poet is to sing into the darkness of our harrowing contemporary lives. Time and again, as she does in early poems like "Requiem" and "Song for Baby-O Unborn," we witness di Prima's capacity for making a stanza of poetry itself a hand in which to hold the quiet sorrow of a muted moment when, in "Minor Arcana," she addresses the mysterious birth and death of Baby-O once again, Baby-O, whose death is certainly no "minor arcana," but instead a source of major mystery, perplexity, and deep pain for the maternal speaker. With a profoundly Zen Buddhist concern for the deceased child, the speaker, now addressing her own mysterious, childless body, almost chants meditatively:

> Body
> whose hands
> broke ground
> for the thrusting head?
> In the eyes
> budding to sight
> who will I read?
>
> Body
> secret in you
>
> sprang this cry of flesh
>
> Now tell the tale. (*Selected Poems*)

In this poem's modest, highly spiritualized and potent final eleven lines, the speaker, exploring, as D.T. Suzuki might say, the "battery" of her own body in which a "mysterious power" was once "latently lying," meditates here upon the death of a child whose body "broke" the consecrated "ground" of her womb only to be buried in earth's "flesh[y]" tomb. In these delicate lines, we hear a speaker struggling to deal with the darker "secrets" of sentient life, meditating on the "cry of the flesh," which is both her own childless, mourning womb, as well as the now near-muted "cry" of Baby-O echoing through her mother's flesh and psyche. Perhaps most significant, though, is the image of "hands" here, which appear time and again in di Prima's Buddhist poetry. Here, as in other poems, interviews, and essays, hands signify for the poet the thrust and force of a direct energy transferred between people, as well as our human capacity to handle and hold other human lives with immense care in a world of undeniable impermanence. Thus, when the poem's speaker asks her "Body" (a body she now feels increasingly estranged from or a deceased child's body now exponentially farther away), "Whose hands / broke ground / for the thrusting head?", we can hear the degree of urgent concern with which the poet wonders about which *precise* sets of human "hands" handled her child's delicate head, either at the moment of conception (breaking the womb's "ground") or at the moment of burial, when the child's body first "broke" the plane of earth and was lowered into ground. Just as in her song for her Baby-O "Unborn," where the poet speaks of the world as a "gutted breaking globe," the image here of a "broke[n] ground" serves to embolden the heart of a Buddhist poetics that emanates a deep compassion toward an inevitably fractured universe, an interminably delicate human hand and frail heart which seek desperately to hold the impossible weight of sorrow.

And yet, for as much as di Prima's and Kandel's poetry seeks to serve as a light hand to hold the weight of darkness, their Buddhist poems also serve as catalysts for letting go of the unmanageable heft of suffering. For if, on one hand, a Buddhist American poet's vocation entails hauling the weight of impermanence, on the other hand Buddhist poet's labor involves the act of crafting a poetry which is firm enough and resolved enough to encourage her reader to let pain go. For in the spirit of Buddha, who cultivated a deep philosophy of non-clinging or non-attachment, di Prima and her Beat compatriot, Kandel, have indeed bequeathed to *us*—their dharmapoetic heirs—a map out of endless burden, a means to release, and be released from the weight of our seemingly inextricable attachments to loved ones, material possessions, and abstract ideas from which we must learn to relinquish our hold. This ethos of psychic release or mental extraction is audible in one of Lenore Kandel's late, previously unpublished poems, where an ostensibly older, wiser Kandel realizes that

> there are times the pressure of possessions
> becomes almost unbearable
> the accumulations of living
> bulwarks of rapturous junk
> I nestle into velvet
> pondering the buoyancy
> of begging bowls
> The cycle always turns for me
> possessions vanish
> gradually I learn
> things or not-things
> it's all alright
> it makes no difference
> things or not-things
> it's all the same. (*Collected Poems*)

Here, in this quintessentially Zen American poem, more closely resembling Diane di Prima's hand-centered poetics of Buddhist, broken-openness, Kandel thoroughly embodies a Buddhism aligned with Shunryu Suzuki Roshi's balanced, Zen teachings. For as much as we might crave the "velvet" comfort of material possessions, Kandel humorously suggests, our desires to possess things we can no longer "hold" or attain ultimately adds "bulwark" weight to our lives. In turn, we wind up striving too eagerly or fervently after a notion of the ascetic life, where a "begging bowl" philosophy of non-attachment itself becomes a kind of self-imposed clinging, an addition of psychic weight, *not* a subtraction of human burden. Here, as in the poetry of di Prima, the metaphor of "holding" becomes not so much a "careless" giving up (as Kandel warns us in "Enlightenment Poem"), but, instead, a reinforcement of the very need for what di Prima has often called "a light touch" of the hand. We must live our lives, these poems seem to say, like Zen artists brush-stroking the canvas of a shared existence with a delicate human calligraphy. On our brushes, on our pens, and on our holds around objects, dreams, and others' lives, we must keep a light grip, for there is nothing here on earth which we ever fully possess. Nor, conversely, should seemingly well-wrought ideas about faith, craft, politics, wealth, or even love, come to possess *us*. For as the contemporary Buddhist American poet Jane Hirshfield herself says in her poem, "A Hand," a hand is not merely "four fingers and a thumb.... Nor is the hand [a body's] meadow of holding, of shaping... / not sponge... / not ink." A hand is "What empties itself" and "falls into the place that is open" (1, 10-11, 13, 16). For Hirshfield, who also meditated in San Francisco, a poet's hand, as it was for her Beat predecessors, is an agent of openness, a means through which to transfer the feathery luminosity of an empty world, a *good* world, an un-"shaped," nonjudgmental, unconditioned world. An ever-possible world.

Or perhaps, the Buddhist, Christian, Sufi, Romantic-inspired living dharma heir, Mary Oliver, has said it best, encapsulating and embodying what di Prima and Kandel have so powerfully, spiritually evoked, in her own Zen poem, "In Blackwater Woods." At last, in the poem's nine concluding lines, Oliver's speaker, meditating on what it means to be human, from a quintessentially Buddhist-American perspective, suggests wisely:

> To live in this world
>
> you must be able
> to do three things:
> to love what is mortal;
> to hold it
>
> against your bones knowing
> your own life depends on it;
> and, when the time comes to let it go,
> to let it go. (*New and Selected Poems: Volume One*)

Here, in some of contemporary poetry's finest lines, an ethos of deep embrace and wide release manifests itself concomitantly within the nine lines of Zen, lyric aphorism. "To live in this world," ancient and modern Buddhist-inspired poets like Li Po, Basho, Muso Soseki, Wallace Stevens, W.S. Merwin, James Wright, Jack Kerouac, Gary Snyder, Allen Ginsberg, Diane di Prima, Lenore Kandel, Anne Waldman, Jane Hirshfield, Mary Oliver, and countless others have radically adopted a spiritopoetic philosophy of the "open hand" and the "swinging door," recognizing that receptivity, spontaneity, egolessness, balance, delicacy, strength, courage, discipline, devotion, empathy, and compassion are all artistic and spiritual cornerstones of a life beautifully, freely, conscientiously, and fruitfully lived. Though Master Taewon and Suzuki Roshi would agree that the road to enlightenment is indeed a "rugged" one, if we "love what is mortal" and "hold it" with grace and care while we are alive, learning to "let" suffering "go" will lighten us and awaken us to the ripples of poetry glimmering now within a stream of endless wonder.

WORKS CITED

Aiken, Richard. "Wallace Stevens and Zen." *The Wallace Stevens Journal* 6.3/4 (1992): 69-73. Print.

Auden, W.H. *Selected Poems*. Ed. Edward Mendelson. New York: Vintage Books, 1979. Print.

Badiner, Allan Hunt. *Dharma Gaia: A Harvest of Essays in Buddhism and Ecology*. Berkeley: Parallax P, 1990. Print.

Baker, Richard. Introduction. *Zen Mind, Beginner's Mind: Informal Talks on Zen Meditation and Practice*. Boston: Shambala, 2011. xiii-xx. Print.

Branaman, Bob. Kali. *San Francisco Oracle: The Psychedelic Newspaper of the Haight Ashbury 1966-1968 (Facsimile Edition)*. Ed. Allen Cohen. Berkeley: Regent P, 1991. 276. Print.

Chadwick, David. *Crooked Cucumber: The Life and Teaching of Shunryu Suzuki*. New York: Broadway Books, 1999. Print.

Charters, Ann. Introduction. "What Was the Beat Generation?" *Beat Down Your Soul: What Was the Beat Generation?* Ed. Ann Charters. New York: Penguin, 2001. Print.

Creeley, Robert. Forward. *Pieces of a Song: Selected Poems*. San Francisco: City Lights Books, 2001. vii. Print.

Culler, Jonathan. *Theory of the Lyric*. Cambridge: Harvard UP, 2015. Print.

Davidson, Michael. *The San Francisco Renaissance: Poets and Community at Mid-Century*. Cambridge: Cambridge UP, 1989. Print.

di Prima, Diane. "By Any Means Necessary." *Beats at Naropa: An Anthology*. Ed.

Anne Waldman and Laura Wright. Minneapolis: Coffee House P, 2009. 195-208. Print.

---. "For Suzuki Roshi." *The Wisdom Anthology of North American Buddhist Poetry.* Ed. Andrew Schelling. Boston: Wisdom Publications, 2005. 61. Print.

---. "I Fail as Dharma Teacher." *The Wisdom Anthology of North American Buddhist Poetry.* Ed. Andrew Schelling. Boston: Wisdom Publications, 2005. 61. Print.

---. "Pieces of a Song: An Interview with Tony Moffett." *Breaking the Rule of Cool: Interviewing and Reading Women Beat Writers.* 29 July 1989. 83-106. Print.

---. *Pieces of a Song: Selected Poems.* San Francisco: City Lights Publishers, 2001. Print.

---. Preface. "Invitation to the Journey: Homage to Lenore Kandel." *Collected Poems of Lenore Kandel.* Berkeley: North Atlantic Books, 2012. xii–xvi. Print.

---. "Tasajara Early 1970's." *The Wisdom Anthology of North American Buddhist Poetry.* Ed. Andrew Schelling. Boston: Wisdom Publications, 2005. 61. Print.

---. "Three 'Dharma' Poems." *The Wisdom Anthology of North American Buddhist Poetry.* Ed. Andrew Schelling. Boston: Wisdom Publications, 2005. 61. Print.

---. "Visit to Katagiri Roshi." Tonkinson, Carole. Ed. *Big Sky Mind: Buddhism and the Beat Generation.* New York: Rutherford Books, 1999. 1-20. Print.

Dresser, Marianne. Introduction. *Buddhist Women on the Edge: Contemporary Perspectives from the Western Frontier.* Ed. Marianne Dresser. Berkeley: North Atlantic Books, 1996. xi-xvii. Print.

Easwaran, Eknath. Introduction. *The Dhammapada.* Trans. Eknath Easwaran. Toronto: Nigiri P, 2007. 13-97. Print.

Eck, Diana. *Darsan: Seeing the Divine Image in India*. New York: Columbia UP, 1998. Print.

Elkholy, Sharin N. Introduction. *The Philosophy of the Beats*. Ed. Sharin Elkholy. Lexington: UP of Kentucky, 2012. 1-7. Print.

Ellwood, Robert. S. *The Fifties Spiritual Marketplace: American Religion in a Decade of Conflict*. New Brunswick, Rutgers UP, 1971. Print.

Ferlinghetti, Lawrence. "Confessional." *Big Sky Mind: Buddhism and the Beat Generation*. Ed. Carole Tonkinson. New York: Rutherford Books, 1999. 1-20. Print.

---. Foreword. *The Collected Poems of Philip Lamantia*. Ed. Garrett Caples, Andrew Joron and Nancy Joyce Peters. Berkley: University of California P, 2013. xiv-xv. Print.

Fields, Rick. *How the Swans Came to the Lake: A Narrative History of Buddhism in America*. Boston: Shambhala, 1992. Print.

Friedrichs, Kurt. "Kali." *The Encyclopedia of Eastern Philosophy and World Religion*. Boston: Shambala, 1986. 170-71. Print.

Ginsberg, Allen. Foreword. *The Beat Book: Writings from the Beat Generation*. Ed. Anne Waldman. Boston. Shambala, 1990. xiii-xvii. Print.

---. *Howl and Other Poems*. San Francisco: City Lights Books, 1956. Print.

Grace, Nancy M. and Ronna C. Johnson. *Breaking the Rule of Cool: Interviewing and Reading Women Beat Writers*. Jackson: UP of Mississippi, 2004. Print.

Gray, Timothy. *Urban Pastoral: Natural Currents in the New York School*. Iowa City: University of Iowa P, 2010. Print.

Haight, Ian. *Garden Chrysanthemums and First Mountain Snow: Zen Questions and Answers from Korea*. Trans. Hongjin Park and Chin' Gak Eryn Reager. Buffalo: White Pine Press, 2010. Print.

Hirshfield, Jane. *Each Happiness Ringed by Lions: Selected Poems*. Glasgow: Bloodaxe Books, 1982. Print.

"In the Great Beyond." *Pressing Concerns for the Study of Religions*. American Academy of Religion. 2004. 14 Feb. 2016. Web.

Johnson, Ronna C. "Lenore Kandel's *The Love Book*: Psychedelic Poetics, Cosmic Erotica, and Sexual Politics in the Mid-Sixties Counterculture." *Reconstructing the Beats*. Ed. Jennie Skerl. New York: Palgrave-McMillan, 2004. 87-104. Print.

Kandel, Lenore. *Collected Poems of Lenore Kandel*. Berkeley: North Atlantic Books, Ed. Anne Waldman. Boston. Shambala, 1990. 275-77. Print.

---. "With Love." *The San Francisco Oracle: The Psychedelic Newspaper of the Haight Asbury 1966-1968 (Facsimile Edition)*. Ed. Allen Cohen. Berkeley: Regent P, 1991. 65. Print.

Knight, Brenda. *Women of the Beat Generation: The Writers, Artists and Muses at the Heart of a Revolution*. Berkeley: Conari P, 1996. Print.

Maitreya, Balangoda Ananda. *The Dhammapada*. U.S.A.: Parallax P, 1995. Print.

McNiece, Ray. Introduction—Part Two. *America Zen: A Gathering of Poets*. Ed. Ray McNiece and Larry Smith. Ohio: Bottom Dog P, 2004. 19-22. Print.

Meyerzove, Lee. "Kandel and McClure: Oracles of Love." *The San Francisco Oracle: The Psychedelic Newspaper of the Haight Ashbury 1966-1968 (Facsimile Edition)*. Ed. Allen Cohen. Berkeley: Regent P, 1991. 65, 83-84. Print.

Oldmeadow, Harry. *Journeys East: Twentieth Century Encounters with Eastern Religious Traditions*. Bloomington: World Wisdom, 2004. Print.

Oliver, Mary. *New and Selected Poems: Volume One*. Boston: Beacon P, 1992. Print.

Olmstead, Mark. "Genius All the Time: The Beats, Spontaneous Presence, and the Primordial Ground." *The Philosophy of the Beats*. Ed. Sharin Elkholy. Lexington: UP of Kentucky, 2012. 179-94. Print.

Pearlman, Ellen. *Nothing and Everything: The Influence of Buddhism on the American Avant-Garde 1942-1962*. Berkley: Evolver Editions, 2012. Print.

Pound, Ezra. *Personae*. New York: New Directions, 1990. Print.

Prothero, Stephen. Introduction. *Big Sky Mind: Buddhism and the Beat Generation*. Ed. Carole Tonkinson. New York: Rutherford Books, 1999. 1-20. Print.

Puchek, Peter. "From Revolution to Creation: Beat Desire and Body Poetics in Anne Waldman's Poetry." *Girls Who Wore Black: Women Writing the Beat Generation*. Ed. Ronna C. Johnson and Nancy M. Grace. New Brunswick: Rutgers UP, 2002. 227-50. Print.

Qian, Zhaoming. "Late Stevens, Nothingness, and the Orient." *The Wallace Stevens Journal* 10.1 (2001): 164-72. Print.

Ritual Trident with the Hindu Deity, Auspicious Kali. 1000-1200. Bronze. Asian Art Museum, San Francisco. Web.

Rubenstein, Steve. "Allen Cohen—Documented Psychedelic Era." *The San Francisco Gate*. 1 May 2004. Web.

Ruskin, Jonah. Interview with Poet Diane di Prima. *San Francisco Gate*. 7 Nov. 2014. Web.

Schneider, Ingrid Fischer. "Dakini." *The Encyclopedia of Eastern Philosophy and World Religion*. Boston: Shambala, 1986. 82-83. Print.

Shields, David and Shane Salerno. *Salinger*. New York: Simon and Schuster, 2013. Print.

Smith, Larry. Introduction. "Outside the Box: Inside the Circle." *America Zen: A Gathering of Poets*. Ed. Ray McNiece and Larry Smith. Ohio: Bottom Dog Press, 2004. 7-18. Print.

Soseki, Muso. *Sun at Midnight*. Trans. W.S. Merwin and Soiku Shigematsu. Washington: Copper Canyon P, 2013. Print.

Stevens, Wallace. *The Collected Poems*. New York: Vintage, New Directions. Print.

Storhoff, Gary and John Whalen-Bridge. Introduction. *The Emergence of Buddhist American Literature.* Ed. Gary Storhoff and John Whalen-Bridge. Albany: SUNY P, 2009. Print.

Suzuki, D.T. *Zen Buddhism: Selected Writings of D.T. Suzuki.* Ed. William Barrett. New York: Three Leaves P, 1996. Print.

Suzuki, Shunryu. *Zen Mind Beginner's Mind: Informal Talks on Zen Meditation and Practice.* Boston: Shambala, 2011. Print.

Tonkinson, Carole. Ed. *Big Sky Mind: Buddhism and the Beat Generation.* New York: Rutherford Books, 1999. 1-20. Print.

Versluis, Arthur. *American Gurus: From Transcendentalism to New Age Religion.* Oxford: Oxford UP, 2014. Print.

Waldman, Anne. "Fast Speaking Woman: An Interview with Ronna Johnson." *Breaking the Rule of Cool: Interviewing and Reading Women Beat Writers.* 3 July 2000. 255-77. Print.

---. "Lenore Kandel." *The Beat Book.* Ed. Anne Waldman. Boston: Shambala P, 1999. 274. Print.

Wallace, David Foster. *This is Water: Some Thoughts Delivered on a Significant Occasion about Living a Compassionate Life.* New York: Little Brown and Company, 2009. Print.

Watts, Alan. *The Way of Zen.* New York: Vintage Books, 1957. Print.

Whitman, Walt. *Leaves of Grass.* New York: Barnes and Noble Classics, 2004. Print.

Williams, William Carlos. Introduction. "Howl for Carl Solomon." *Howl and Other Poems.* San Francisco: City Lights Books, 1956. 7-8. Print.

Wright, James. *The Branch Will Not Break.* Hanover: Wesleyan UP, 1963. Print.

www.ingramcontent.com/pod-product-compliance
Lightning Source LLC
Chambersburg PA
CBHW070422010526
44118CB00014B/1870